PRAGUE

THEODORE SCHWINKE

Left **View from Petřín Hill** Right **Holocaust Memorial Wall, Pinkas Synagogue**

LONDON, NEW YORK,
MELBOURNE, MUNICH AND DELHI
www.dk.com

Produced by Sargasso Media Ltd, London

Reproduced by Colourscan, Singapore
Printed and bound in China by Leo Paper
Products Ltd

First published in Great Britain in 2003 by
Dorling Kindersley Limited
80 Strand, London WC2R 0RL
A Penguin Company

**Copyright 2003, 2007, 2009 © Dorling
Kindersley Limited, London
Reprinted with revisions 2005, 2009**

A CIP catalogue record is available from the
British Library.

ISBN 978 1 40533 353 5

Within each Top 10 list in this book, no
hierarchy of quality or popularity is implied.
All 10 are, in the editor's opinion, of roughly
equal merit.

Contents

Prague's Top 10

Share your travel recommendations on traveldk.com

Left **Communist Memorial, Wenceslas Square** Right **Modern Bohemian crystal**

Left **The Loreto** Right **St Wenceslas mural, Storch House**

Key to abbreviations
Adm admission charge **Free** no admission charge **Dis. access** disabled access

3

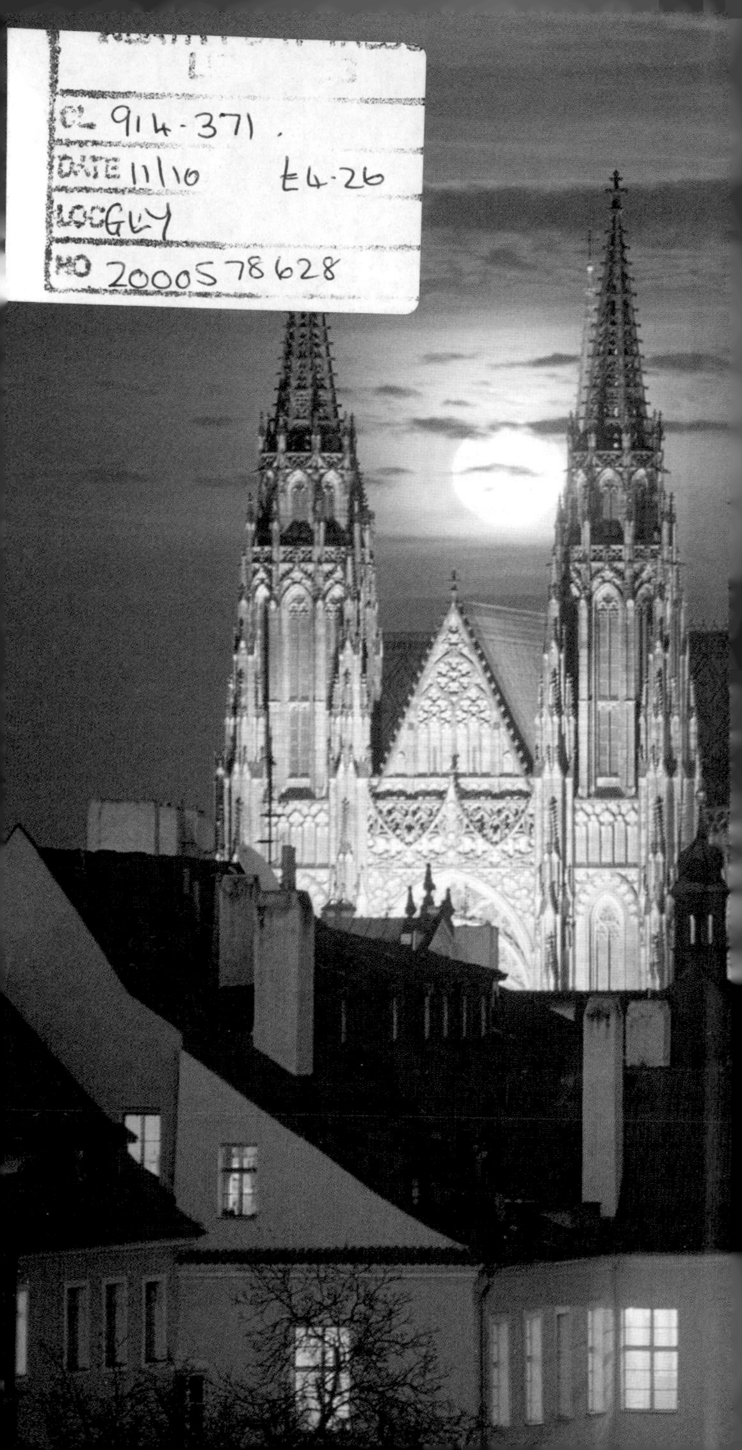

PRAGUE'S
TOP 10

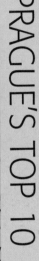

PRAGUE'S TOP 10

🔟 Prague's Highlights

At the geographical heart of Europe, Prague's beautiful cityscape has been carved and sustained by a variety of emperors, artists and religious communities, from the Gothic exuberance of its castle and cathedral, to the dignity of the medieval Jewish Cemetery, and the 19th-century opulence of the "new" town. Under Communist rule, Prague was off the tourist map, but since 1989 the city has seen a surge of visitors eager to take in this spectacular city.

1 Prague Castle

The hilltop fortress of the Přemyslids is home to the head of the Czech Republic. Spend a day exploring the castle's many impressive palaces, churches, galleries and gardens *(see pp8–11)*.

St Vitus's Cathedral 2

The glory of the castle complex, St Vitus's took more than 500 years to build. Climb its southern tower for wonderful views of Prague, or visit its crypt to see the tombs of Bohemia's Holy Roman Emperors *(see pp12–13)*.

3 Old Town Square

Prague's central square has been a market since the Middle Ages, and was witness to the rise and fall of numerous regimes and no shortage of bloodshed. The city has few charms finer than watching the moon rise between the towers of the Church of Our Lady Before Týn *(see pp14–17)*.

4 Charles Bridge

Linking the city across the River Vltava, it can be difficult to appreciate the beautiful carved statues of former citizens, due to the incessant crowds and trinket stalls. But it's worth the effort *(see pp18–19)*.

5 The Loreto
Pilgrims have visited this Baroque shrine to the Virgin Mary since the 17th century. Visitors can see priceless ornaments in its treasury *(see pp20–21).*

6 Old Jewish Cemetery
The jumble of tombstones in this tiny graveyard give some indication of the number of bodies buried here. Prague's Jewish community lived and worshipped in the surrounding ghetto *(see pp22–5).*

7 National Gallery
One of the first Functionalist buildings in Europe, the Trade Fair Palace now houses the National Gallery's collection of modern and contemporary art, including 14 Picassos *(see pp26–7).*

8 St Agnes's Convent
Prague's oldest Gothic building is now home to the National Gallery's collection of medieval art and remains a monument to its founder, a Přemyslid princess who gave up a life at court to pursue her faith *(see pp28–9).*

10 Petřín Hill
Perched above Malá Strana, the forested Petřín Hill is criss-crossed with footpaths, giving visitors some of the finest views in the city. The old Ukrainian church is wonderfully romantic *(see pp32–3).*

9 Wenceslas Square
From its origins as a humble horse market, Wenceslas Square has grown into a modern business centre. Monuments on the square remind visitors of its role in the nation's tumultuous history *(see pp30–31).*

TOP 10 Prague Castle

Crowned by the distinct spires of St Vitus's Cathedral (see pp12–13), Prague Castle (Pražský Hrad) is the metaphorical and historical throne of the Czech lands. Prince Bořivoj built a wooden fortress here in the late 9th century, establishing the hilltop overlooking the river as the Přemyslid's dynastic seat. The castle later became the capital of the Holy Roman Empire. Much of the castle was rebuilt in the 16th century, resulting in the glorious Renaissance edifice seen today. Today it is home to the President of the Czech Republic.

Main entrance

⭐ The Castle Guard changes every day at noon, but the big show is on Sundays.

At 10am each day a brass quartet serenades Malá Strana from a pavilion overlooking the Old Castle Steps.

- Hradčany, Prague 1
- Map C2
- 224 373368
- www.hrad.cz
- Castle grounds: Open Apr–Oct: 5am–midnight daily, Nov–Mar: 6am–11pm daily; Royal Palace: Open Apr–Oct: 9am–5pm daily, Nov–Mar: 9am–4pm daily; St George's Convent: Open 10am–6pm Tue–Sun; St George's Basilica: Open Apr–Oct: 9am–5pm daily, Nov–Mar: 9am– 4pm daily
- Adm Kč350 (includes St George's Basilica, Powder Tower and Old Royal Palace)

Top 10 Features

1. Old Royal Palace
2. Gardens on the Ramparts
3. Summer Gardens
4. Battling Titans
5. St George's Convent
6. St George's Basilica
7. White Tower
8. Powder Tower
9. Golden Lane
10. Daliborka

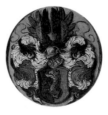

1 Old Royal Palace
While Prince Bořivoj made do with a wooden structure, subsequent residences were built on top of each other as the tastes of Bohemia's rulers changed *(see pp10–11)*. Halls are decorated with coats of arms *(above)*.

2 Gardens on the Ramparts
Ferdinand I and his son Maximilian II gave the dour castle some greenery in the late 16th century, and the First Republic architect Josip Plečnik created the lined paths, steps and grottoes that extend to Malá Strana *(right)*.

3 Summer Gardens
Ferdinand I also created these "pleasure gardens" for his wife Anne. Italian in style, they included a maze, a zoo, and the Belvedere.

➜ *For more sights around Hradčany See pp90–93*

4 Battling Titans
These stone giants have dominated the First Courtyard since Empress Maria Theresa asked Ignatz Platzer to sculpt them in the 18th century.

5 St George's Convent
Princess Mlada established the first Czech convent here in the 10th century. The Romanesque building now houses 19th-century Czech art.

Plan of Prague Castle

9 Golden Lane
The colourful hovels *(below)* built into the castle wall were home to goldsmiths so they could avoid guild dues in town.

10 Daliborka
Dalibor, something of a Czech Robin Hood, was captured and became the first prisoner of the tower that now takes his name *(below)*.

6 St George's Basilica
Prince Vratislav built the basilica in AD 921. The chapel of St Wenceslas's grandmother, St Ludmila, is decorated with beautiful 16th-century paintings *(below)*.

7 White Tower
The White Tower contains a torture chamber and, today, shops selling grisly souvenirs. The gangways from which archers once watched over the moat are lined with replicas of weapons.

8 Powder Tower
This was Rudolf II's top research facility, where alchemists sought the Philosopher's Stone. Oddly, the Czech name *"mihulka"* implies a place where lampreys are kept.

Castle Guide
You can wander through much of the castle complex for free, but to see the interiors, buy a ticket at the tourist office in the third courtyard. One admission fee gains access to the Old Royal Palace, St George's convent and basilica and the Powder Tower. A separate fee admits you to St Vitus, Golden Lane or other parts of the castle.

Left **Bohemian Chancellery** Right **Land Rolls**

TOP10 Features of the Royal Palace

1 Vladislav Hall

Benedict Ried created a mastery of Gothic design with his elaborate vaulting here. Since the First Republic, the country's presidents have been ceremoniously chosen here, but it has also been used for coronations and jousting tournaments.

2 Riders' Staircase

The low steps and vaulted ceiling of this stairway permitted mounted knights to make spectacular entrances to tournaments held in Vladislav Hall.

3 Louis Wing

Only 10 years and a few steps separate the southern wing from the main hall, but in the interim, Benedict Ried moved castle architecture from Gothic to Renaissance. Bohemian nobles met here in an administrative body when the king was away.

The Diet

4 Bohemian Chancellery

The first battle of the Thirty Years' War was staged here. Protestant noblemen threw two Catholic governors and their secretary from the east window. Their fall was broken by a dung heap – or an intervening angel, depending on whom you ask.

5 Land Rolls

The coats of arms decorating the walls belong to clerks who kept tabs on property ownership and court decisions from 1614 to 1777. Until the reign of Maria Theresa, record books were not numbered, but identified by elaborate covers.

6 Diet

Bohemian nobles met here with the king in a prototype parliament. The king sat on the throne (the one seen today is a 19th-century replica), the archbishop sat to the king's right, while the estates sat on his left. The portraits on the wall show, from the left, Maria Theresa, her husband Franz, Josef II, Leopold II and Franz I, who fought Napoleon at Austerlitz.

Riders' Staircase

7 Chapel of All Saints
At the eastern end of Vladislav Hall, a doorway leads to a balcony above the Chapel of All Saints. Peter Parler modelled it on the Gothic Sainte-Chapelle in Paris. After fire destroyed it in 1541, it was redesigned in Baroque style. Of particular artistic note is Hans von Aachen's *Triptych of the Angels*.

8 Soběslav Residence
Prince Soběslav literally laid the foundations for Prague Castle, building the first stone palace here in the 11th century.

9 Gothic and Romanesque Cellars
These rooms became buried as a result of subsequent construction overhead. A replica of the crown jewels is on display; the real thing was kept here during World War II.

10 Busts from Peter Parléř's Workshop
These impressive portraits were created in the late 14th century and include the grandfather-father-grandson set of John of Luxembourg, Charles IV and Wenceslas IV.

Top 10 Rulers of Prague
1. Wenceslas (birthdate unknown–935)
2. Otakar II (1233–78)
3. Charles IV (1316–78)
4. Wenceslas IV (1361–1419)
5. Rudolph II (1552–1612)
6. Tomáš Garrigue Masaryk (1850–1937)
7. Edvard Beneš (1884–1948)
8. Klement Gottwald (1896–1953)
9. Alexander Dubček (1921–92)
10. Václav Havel (b.1936)

Prague's Third Defenestration

Prague's first recorded instance of execution by hurling the condemned from a window occurred at the outset of the Hussite Wars in 1419. Vladislav II's officials met a similar fate in 1483. Perhaps as a tribute to their forebears, more than 100 Protestant nobles stormed the Old Royal Palace in 1618 and cast two hated Catholic governors and their secretary out of the window. The men's fall was broken by a dung heap swept from the Vladislav Hall after a recent tournament (although Catholics at the time claim they were saved by angels). The incident is often cited as the spark that began the Thirty Years' War. Following the Protestants' defeat at Bílá Hora in 1620, the nobles got their day in court and at the gallows, in front of the Old Town Hall (see pp16–17).

Prague's Defenestration
This 1889 work by Václav von Brožik captures the moment of the Protestants' attack on the Catholic governors. Painted 250 years later, it illustrates how the event has remained in the Czech consciousness.

St Vitus's Cathedral

This spectacular Gothic cathedral is an unmissable sight in Prague, not least because of its dominant position on Hradčany hill, looming over the Vltava and the rest of the city. Prince Wenceslas first built a rotunda here upon a pagan worship site and dedicated it to St Vitus (svatý Vít), a Roman saint. Matthew d'Arras began work on the grand cathedral in 1344 when Prague was named an archbishopric. He died shortly thereafter and Charles IV hired the Swabian wunderkind Peter Parléř to take over. With the intervention of the Hussite Wars, however, work stopped and, remarkably, construction was only finally completed in 1929.

Great Tower windows

🕙 Much of St Vitus's Cathedral can be appreciated for free. Seeing all that the cathedral and the castle have to offer can take a whole day.

- *Third Courtyard, Prague Castle*
- *Map C2*
- *www.katedralapraha.cz*
- *Open Apr–Oct: 9am–5pm Mon–Sat, noon–5pm Sun; Nov–Mar: 9am–4pm daily*
- *Nave: Free; St Vitus's Cathedral, St George's Basilica, Powder Tower & Royal Palace: Adm Kč350*

Top 10 Features

1. South Tower
2. Wenceslas Chapel
3. Crown Jewels
4. Royal Crypt
5. Royal Oratory
6. St John of Nepomuk's Tomb
7. New Archbishop's Chapel
8. Sigismund
9. Golden Portal
10. High Altar

South Tower
Visitors can clearly see at exactly which point the Hussite civil wars put a stop to construction of this 96-m (315-ft) tower. By the time work resumed, architectural style had moved into the Renaissance, hence the incongruous rounded cap on a Gothic base.

Wenceslas Chapel
This chapel *(left)* stands where Prince Wenceslas built the first St Vitus rotunda and contains the tomb of its namesake, Bohemia's patron saint. The frescoes of Christ's Passion on the lower wall are surrounded by 1,300 semi-precious stones. Vladislav II commissioned the upper frescoes of St Wenceslas's life, painted to celebrate his son Ludvik's coronation.

For more places of worship in Prague See pp38–9

Crown Jewels

3 You would think there would be safer places for the crown and sceptre of Bohemia, but the coronation chamber above Wenceslas Chapel is said to be guarded by the spirit of the saint.

St John of Nepomuk's Tomb

6 The silver for this 1,680-kg (3,700-lb) coffin *(above)* came from the Bohemian mining town of Kutná Hora, symbolized by the statues of miners to the left of the tomb.

New Archbishop's Chapel

7 Alfons Mucha created the Art Nouveau window of the Slavic saints for the Archbishop's Chapel *(below)*. Despite appearances, the glass is painted, not stained.

Sigismund

8 The 16-tonne bell of the Great Tower *(below)*, affectionately known as Sigismund, is the nation's largest and dates from 1549. It takes four volunteers to ring the bell on important church holidays and events.

Royal Crypt

4 The greatest kings of Bohemia are buried in a single room beneath the cathedral, including Charles IV, Wenceslas IV and Rudolf II.

Royal Oratory

5 The royal family crossed a narrow bridge from the Royal Palace *(see p8)* to this private gallery to hear mass. The coats of arms represent all the countries that were ruled by Vladislav II.

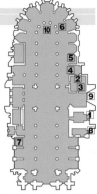

Cathedral Floorplan

Golden Portal

9 This triple-arched arcade *(above)* was the main entrance to the cathedral until the western end was completed in the 20th century.

High Altar

10 Bounded by St Vitus's Chapel and the marble sarcophagi of Ferdinand I and family, the high altar and chancel *(centre)* follow a strict Neo-Gothic philosophy.

Peter Parléř

After the death of Matthew d'Arras, Charles IV made Parléř his chief architect. Parléř undertook St Vitus's Cathedral, Charles Bridge and numerous other Gothic monuments which still stand in Prague. He trained the artisans and his talented sons and nephews continued his work after his death in 1399.

TOP 10 Old Town Square

As the heart and soul of the city, no visitor should, or is likely to miss the Old Town Square (Staroměstské náměstí). A marketplace was located here in the 11th century, but it was in 1338, when John of Luxembourg gave Prague's burghers permission to form a town council, that the Old Town Hall was built (see p16) and the square came into its own. Today, it has a lively atmosphere, with café tables set out in front of painted façades, horses and carts waiting to ferry tourists around the city and street-sellers hawking their wares.

Jan Hus Memorial

🍺 The cheapest beer on the square, aside from that in plastic cups, is at U Mravence, U Radnice 20, north of the Old Town Hall.

⏱ Resist the temptation to climb on the Jan Hus Monument. Doing so, or trampling the flowers will earn you a fine, as well as embarrassment.

• Map M3 • Old Town Hall: 724 508584; Open Apr–Oct: 11am–6pm Mon, 9am–6pm Tue–Sun, Nov–Mar: 11am–5pm Mon, 9am–5pm Tue–Sun Adm Kč60

Top 10 Features

1. Dům u Minuty
2. House at the Stone Bell
3. Church of Our Lady Before Týn
4. Church of St Nicholas
5. Jan Hus Memorial
6. Marian Column
7. Ungelt
8. Štorch House
9. Golz-Kinský Palace
10. Malé náměstí

1 Dům u Minuty
The "House at the Minutes" *(above)* probably takes its name from the not-so-minute *sgraffito* images on its walls. The alchemical symbols adorning Staroměstské náměstí 2 date from 1611. Franz Kafka lived in the black-and-white house as a boy *(see p44)*.

2 House at the Stone Bell
Formerly done up in Baroque style, workers discovered the Gothic façade of this house as late as 1980. On the southwestern corner is the the bell which gives the house its name. The Municipal Gallery often hosts temporary exhibitions here.

3 Church of Our Lady Before Týn
This Gothic edifice *(below)* began as a humble church serving residents in the mercantile town *(týn)* in the 14th century. Following architectural conventions of the time, the south tower is stouter than the north one.

Church of St Nicholas
Prague has two Baroque churches of St Nicholas, both built by Kilian Ignac Dientzenhoffer. The architect completed the one in Old Town *(right)* two years before starting Malá Strana's *(see p82)*. Regular concerts here give visitors a chance to hear the church's organ.

Malé náměstí
The ornate well in the centre of the "Small Square" doubles as a plague memorial. The elaborate murals of craftsmen on the façade of Rott House *(below)* are the only decoration now left. Until the early 1990s, the building was a hardware store.

Jan Hus Memorial
Hus was burned at the stake in 1415 for proposing radical Church reform. The inscription below the figure of Hus reads "Truth Will Prevail".

Marian Column
On Czechoslovakia's declaration of independence in 1918, this former column reminded jubilant mobs of Habsburg rule and they tore it down. A plan is afoot to rebuild it.

Ungelt
The courtyard behind Týn church was home to foreign merchants in the 14th century, but today it is home to smart boutiques and cafés.

Štorch House
An Art Nouveau equestrian painting of St Wenceslas is the focal point of the house at Staroměstské náměstí 18.

Golz-Kinský Palace
Once occupied by Communists, this former palace *(centre & below)* now houses the National Gallery's collection of prints and drawings and an up-market restaurant.

Jan Hus

The rector of Prague (later Charles) University, Jan Hus was dedicated to fighting against corruption in the Church. He was declared a heretic by the Church, and was summoned to Germany where he was burned at the stake. Czech resentment turned into civil war, with Hussite rebels facing the power of Rome. But the Hussites split into moderate and radical factions, the former defeating the latter in 1434. Hus is still a national figure – 6th July, the day he was killed, is a public holiday.

Left **Apostles** Centre **Crosses, White Mountain Memorial** Right **Gothic Chapel**

10 Old Town Hall Features

1 Astronomical Clock
During the day, on the hour, bells ring, cocks crow and 15th-century statues dance while the necks of tourists below stiffen.

2 Apostles
Marionette artist Vojtěch Sucharda sculpted the 12 wooden figures that turn out for the crowds on the astronomical clock – they replace the ones destroyed by German artillery in 1945. A brochure identifies which saint is which.

3 Art Gallery
On the Old Town Hall's ground floor is an exhibition space which features temporary shows.

4 Dukla Memorial
Behind a brass plaque identified by the year "1945" is a pot of soil from the Dukla battle-field. German artillery gunned down 84,000 Red Army soldiers in this Slovak pass in one of the most grievous military miscalculations of World War II.

5 White Mountain Memorial
Twenty-seven crosses are set in the pavement on the town hall's eastern side in memory of the Bohemian nobles who were executed for their role in the Thirty Years' War (see p34). After Protestant forces were defeated at the Battle of White Mountain, the men were hanged, beheaded or drawn and quartered here in a public ceremony.

6 Gothic Chapel
The small chapel adjoining the Mayors' Hall was consecrated in 1381 in honour of the saints Wenceslas, Vitus and Ludmila. Wenceslas IV's emblem and his wife Eufemia's initial adorn the entrance portal. In the nave is a scale model of the Marian column which stood on the Old Town Square until 1918 and may be rebuilt (see p15).

7 Elevator
The elevator taking visitors up to the viewing gallery of the tower won an award for best design in 1999. Oddly enough, its space-age design works harmoniously within the stony surroundings. It also permits wheelchair access to the top of the tower – a rare consideration in Prague.

Church of St Nicholas seen from the Viewing Gallery

While you're enjoying the hourly astronomical clock performance, keep an eye on your wallet as well as the show

Viewing Gallery

The parapet under the Old Town Hall's roof affords visitors a unique view of the square and the Old Town below. Bring your pocket change: Kč20 will buy you two minutes on a miniature telescope, with which you can admire the entire Prague Valley.

Craft stalls lining The Green

Gothic Cellars

The cellars of the Old Town Hall were once ground floor rooms. The town was subject to flooding, so more earth was added to keep burghers' feet dry. The spaces were used as granaries and debtors' prisons.

The Green

Retreating German artillery unloaded their guns on the Old Town Hall's north wing to avoid carrying the shells back to Berlin. After the war, the wing was torn down. Now the area is lined with stalls selling Czech handicrafts.

Top 10 Features of the Astronomical Clock

1. Solar clock
2. Lunar clock
3. Josef Mánes Calendar
4. Apostles
5. Angel and the Sciences
6. Vanity, Avarice, Death and Lust
7. Rooster
8. Hourly Shows
9. Master Hanuš
10. Dial

Building the Old Town Hall

Prague's Old Town received its charter and fortifications from John of Luxembourg in the mid-13th century, but its town clerk had to wait nearly 150 years for an office. The Old Town Hall was cobbled together from existing houses over the centuries until it comprised the five houses that stand at Staroměstské náměstí 1–2 today. The hall's eastern wing once stretched to within a few feet of the door of the Church of St Nicholas (see p15), but German artillery reduced it to rubble in 1945. The clock tower was installed in 1410, but the clock wasn't up and running until 1572.

Medieval Astrology

The Astronomical Clock's face not only tells the current time, but relates the movement of the planets around earth and the sun and moon through the signs of the zodiac. It is decorated with paintings by Josef Mánes.

Charles Bridge

The spectacular Charles Bridge (Karlův most) has witnessed more than 600 years of processions, battles, executions and, increasingly, film shoots. Peter Parléř (see p13) built the viaduct to replace its predecessor, the Judith Bridge, in Gothic style. The bridge's most distinguishing feature is its gallery of 30 statues. The saints and other religious figures were installed, from 1683 onwards, to lead the masses back to mass. Some, such as Braun's St Luitgard, are incomparably lovely; others, such as Bohn's Calvary, are politically controversial. Today all the statues are reproductions – the originals are preserved in museums across the city.

Old Town Bridge Tower detail

🖙 The Malá Strana bridge tower houses an exhibit on the bridge's history. It is Open Apr–Oct 10am–6pm daily.

• Map J4

Top 10 Features

1. Old Town Bridge Tower
2. Calvary
3. The Lorraine Cross
4. Statue of St John of Nepomuk
5. Statue of Sts Cyril and Methodius
6. Statue of Bruncvik
7. Our Lady of the Mangles
8. Statue of St Luitgard
9. Antonin
10. Statue of the Trinitarian Order

1 Old Town Bridge Tower

From the parapet of the Old Town bridge tower, you can see the gentle S-curve that the architect Peter Parléř built into the viaduct to obstruct invaders, as well as a jaw-dropping panorama of the city.

2 Calvary

This statue *(right)* will cause double-takes among students of Hebrew. According to a nearby apologia, the words "Holy, holy, holy is the Lord of Hosts" were added in 1696, paid for by a local Jewish man who had been accused of profaning the cross.

3 The Lorraine Cross

Halfway across the bridge is a brass cross where John Nepomuk's body was thrown into the river *(see p35)*. It is said that if you wish on the cross the wish will come true.

Statue of St John of Nepomuk 4
Rubbing the brass relief *(right)* of the saint shown diving into the river is an old tradition, thought to bring good luck; petting the adjacent brass dog is a new one.

Statue of St Luitgard 8
Matthias Brauns' 1710 depiction of a blind nun's dream, in which the crucified Christ permitted her to touch his wounds *(below)*, retains a timeless appeal.

Statue of Bruncvik 6
Peer over the bridge's southern edge to see the Czech's answer to King Arthur. Bruncvik and his army are promised to awaken and save Prague at the city's most desperate hour.

Antonin 9
One of many artists selling work from the bridge, Antonin paints portraits of himself as the devil. His proximity to the Čertovka (Devil's Canal) may be the key.

Our Lady of the Mangles 7
The portrait of Mary hanging on the house south of the bridge *(above)* is tied to an ancient tale of miraculous healing. Seeing the light go out on the balcony below is supposedly an omen of imminent death – don't stare too long.

Statue of the Trinitarian Order 10
This religious order was set up to ransom prisoners of war from the Crusades and buy Christians their freedom; hence the bored Turk guarding the cell.

When to Visit Charles Bridge

During summer, and increasingly year-round, the bridge is well nigh impassable throughout the day, crowded with artists, tourists and the odd Dixieland jazz band. It's best seen in the early hours as the sun rises over the Old Town bridge tower. A late evening stroll gives a similarly dramatic view, with the illuminated St Nicholas's Church and castle looming above.

Statue of Sts Cyril and Methodius 5
Greek missionaries who brought both Christianity and the Cyrillic alphabet to the Czech lands, Cyril and Methodius are national heroes to this day. Karel Dvořák created this statue *(right)* in 1928 at the peak of Czechoslovakia's period of National Awakening, following independence.

🔟 The Loreto

At the heart of this sparkling 17th-century Baroque pilgrimage site is its claim to fame and most proud possession: a replica of the original Santa Casa in Loreto, Italy, believed to be the house where the Virgin Mary received the Incarnation. Construction of the grandiose church and the surrounding chapels coincided with the Counter Reformation, and one of Prague's first Baroque buildings was intended to lure Czechs back to the Catholic faith.

Loreto entrance

🔵 Just around the corner from the Loreto, at Kapucínská 2, is a monument to people tortured by the secret police at the former Interior Ministry building.

- Loretánské náměstí 7
- Map A2
- 220 516740
- www.loreta.cz
- Open 9am–12:15pm, 1–4:30pm Tue–Sun
- Adm Kč110

Top 10 Features

1. Loretánské náměstí
2. Santa Casa
3. Belltower
4. Outer Courtyard
5. Arcade
6. St Wilgifortis Altar
7. Church of the Nativity
8. Altars of SS Felissimus and Marcia
9. Treasury
10. Diamond Monstrance

1 Loretánské náměstí

This square is said to have been a pagan burial ground. The stucco façade of the Loreto *(above)* is dwarfed by the Černin Palace opposite, home of the Ministry of Foreign Affairs.

2 Santa Casa

The stucco reliefs on the outside of this replica of the Holy Family's house in Nazareth depict scenes from the Virgin Mary's life. Inside is the miracle-working statue of Our Lady of Loreto.

3 Belltower

The carillon *(below)* was the gift of a Prague merchant whose daughter was healed by the intercession of the Lady of Loreto. An automated mechanism chimes a Marian hymn every hour.

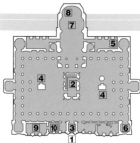

Plan of The Loreto

4 Inner Courtyard

In the inner courtyard, visitors can admire two Baroque fountains. The north fountain features a sculpture of the Resurrection; the south, the Assumption of the Virgin Mary *(right)*.

9 Treasury

The Communists crafted this exhibit of sacred gold and silver items to show how peasants were brought to obedience with this "cheap promise of happiness beyond the grave."

10 Diamond Monstrance

The silver work by Johann Bernard Fischer von Erlach is covered with 6,222 diamonds. The Virgin looks up at her son, represented by the host in the receptacle.

Santa Casa

The Santa Casa was the Nazareth house in which the archangel Gabriel is believed to have announced to the Virgin Mary that she would conceive the Son of God. In the 13th century, the Greek Angeli family moved the house to Loreto, Italy. As the Marian cult spread, copies of the Loreto started emerging all over Europe – the Prague site *(below)* is believed to be the truest representation of the original.

5 Arcade

Before and after visiting the Santa Casa, pilgrims passed through the arcade and prayed at its chapels of St Anne, St Francis Seraphim, the Holy Family, the Holy Rood, St Antony of Padua and Our Lady of Sorrows.

6 St Wilgifortis Altar

The Chapel of Our Lady of Sorrows is dominated by the sight of a crucified, bearded woman. St Wilgifortis was a Portuguese maiden who prayed for a masculine appearance to preserve her chastity.

7 Church of the Nativity

Originally a small alcove behind the Santa Casa, the church was expanded into its present size in 1717. The Rococo organ stands opposite the altar, over a crypt to Loreto benefactors.

8 Altars of SS Felicissimus and Marcia

On either side of the altar in the Church of the Nativity are large reliquary displays containing the remains of these two Spanish saints.

Old Jewish Cemetery

The crumbling image of the Old Jewish Cemetery is a moving memorial to Prague's once considerable Jewish community. As this was one of the few burial sites available to Prague's Jews, when the plot was full, graves built up in layers – estimates put the number at about 200,000, with the oldest headstone dating from 1439. The final burial took place in 1787, but stroll through the enclosure and you'll get a sense of noble lives once lived.

Rabbi Loew's Grave

🌀 It is customary for men to wear a *yarmulka* (skull cap) in the synagogues. Look for them near the entrance, but return it when you leave.

The Museum of Decorative Arts' east-facing windows offer an excellent crowd-free view of the cemetery *(see p37)*.

• Old Jewish Cemetery: U Starého hřbitova, Map K3, 224 819456, www.jewishmuseum.cz, Open Apr–Oct: 9am–6pm Sun–Fri; Nov– Mar: 9am–4:30pm; Closed Jewish holidays, Adm Kč300 (includes entrance to various synagogues).
• Old-New Synagogue: Pařižská, Map K3, Open 9:30am–6pm Sun–Fri (to 5pm Nov–Mar) Adm Kč200

Top 10 Features

1. Avigdor Kara's Grave
2. Mordecai Maisel's Grave
3. Rabbi Loew's Grave
4. David Gans's Tombstone
5. Klausen Synagogue
6. Rabbi Oppenheim's Grave
7. Gothic Tombstones
8. Hendl Bashevi's Grave
9. Zemach Graves
10. Nephele Mound

1 Avigdor Kara's Grave
The oldest grave is that of this poet and scholar, best known for his documentation of the pogrom of 1389, which he survived as a child.

2 Mordecai Maisel's Grave
Mordecai Maisel (1528–1601) was ghetto mayor during the reign of Rudolf II, and funded the synagogue that bears his name *(see p100)*.

3 Rabbi Loew's Grave
The burial site of one of Prague's major Jewish figures, Rabbi Jehuda Loew ben Bezalel (1520–1609), and creator of the Golem *(see p52)*.

4 David Gans's Tombstone
A pupil of Rabbi Loew, Gans (1541–1613) was the author of a seminal two-volume history of the Jewish people. He was also an accomplished astronomer during the time of Johannes Kepler *(see p35)*. His headstone *(right)* is marked with the Star of David, after his name and his faith.

5 Klausen Synagogue
Mordechai Maisel also commissioned the building of the Klausen Synagogue *(left)* on the cemetery's northern edge. It now houses exhibitions on Jewish festivals and traditions.

Rabbi Oppenheim's Grave

Rabbi David Oppenheim *(left)* was the first chief rabbi of Moravia, and later chief rabbi of Bohemia and finally of Prague, where he died in 1734.

Plan of the Old Jewish Cemetery

Entrance

Zemach Graves

Next to the Pinkas Synagogue *(see p101)* is a square gravestone where Mordechai Zemach (d. 1592) is buried with his son Bezalel (d. 1589). The name Zemach means "spring" in Hebrew.

Nephele Mound

Stillborn children, miscarried babies and other infants who died under a year old were buried in the southeast corner of the cemetery.

Hendl Bashevi's Grave

This elaborate tombstone *(below)* marks the resting place of the so-called "Jewish Queen", Hendl Bashevi. Her husband, mayor Jacob Bashevi, was knighted and permitted a coat of arms, seen on his wife's gravestone.

Gothic Tombstones

The eastern wall of the cemetery holds fragments of Gothic tombstones *(above)* rescued in 1866 from another graveyard near Vladislavova street. Further graves at another site were uncovered in the 1990s.

Grave Symbols

As a rule, a Hebrew tombstone *(matzevah)* contains the deceased's name, date of death and eulogy. In addition to these basics, the grave-markers in the Old Jewish Cemetery often included symbolic images indicating the deceased's lineage. Names are often symbolized by animals, according to Biblical precedent or Hebrew or Germanic translations – David Gans's tombstone features a goose *(gans* in German). Some professions are also represented: scissors may appear on a tailor's tombstone, for example.

Left **Façade** Centre **Vaulting** Right **Nave**

🔟 Features in the Old-New Synagogue

1 Rabbi Loew's Chair
Topped with a Star of David, the tall chair found by the eastern wall has been reserved for Prague's chief rabbis throughout the synagogue's history.

2 Jewish Standard
Prague's Jewish community was permitted a banner in the 15th century as a symbol of its autonomy. The copy hanging above the Bimah replicates a 1716 original, featuring a Jewish hat within a six-pointed star and the legend *"Shema Yisroel"*.

Rabbi Loew's Chair

3 Nave
Twelve narrow windows, evoking the 12 tribes of Israel, line the perimeter walls, which are unadorned, save for the abbreviation of Biblical verses. Two central pillars are modelled on the façade columns of the Temple of Jerusalem.

4 Ark
Behind the curtain on the eastern wall are the Torah scrolls, which are kept in the holy ark. The tympanum features foliage and grape motifs, also found in nearby St Agnes's Convent *(see pp28–9)*, and date from the synagogue's construction in the late 13th century.

5 Entrance
The Biblical inscription "Revere God and observe His commandments! For this applies to all mankind" admonished worshippers entering and leaving the synagogue.

6 Vaulting
To avoid the sign of the cross, a fifth rib was added to the nave's vaulting, decorated with vine leaves and ivy.

7 Women's Windows
Women were not permitted in the nave of the synagogue, but sat in the vestibule. Narrow openings in the wall allowed them to follow the services.

8 Bimah
A pulpit stands on this dais in the centre. From here the rabbi reads the Torah and performs wedding ceremonies.

9 Attic
Legend has it that Rabbi Loew stashed the remains of the Golem *(see p52)* under the synagogue's large saddle roof.

10 Josefov Town Hall
Adjacent to the synagogue is the Jewish Town Hall. The façade clock's hands run counter-clockwise – or clockwise, if you read Hebrew *(see p99)*.

For more Places of Worship **See pp38–9**

Top 10 Jewish Leaders

1 Eliezer ben Elijah Ashkenazi (1513–86)
2 Judah Loew ben Bezalel (1525–1609)
3 Mordecai Maisel (1528–1601)
4 Mordecai ben Abraham Jaffe (1535–1612)
5 Ephraim Solomon ben Aaron of Lunshits (1550–1619)
6 Joseph Solomon Delmedigo (1591–1655)
7 David ben Abraham Oppenheim (1664–1736)
8 Ezekiel ben Judah Landau (1713–93)
9 Solomon Judah Lieb Rapoport (1790–1867)
10 Efraim Karol Sidon (b. 1942)

Prague Ghetto
During World War II, Prague's Jews were moved to a town called Terezín, where religious practices were banned.

The Jews in Prague

Prague's Jews have been plagued by anti-Semitic behaviour almost since their arrival in the 10th century. Zealous Christians destroyed an early settlement in what is now Malá Strana. Such pogroms were not uncommon – the most infamous is the Passover slaughter of 1389, in which rioters killed more than 3,000 Jews, including those who had taken refuge in the Old-New Synagogue. But there were high points. Prominent Jews – notably Rabbi Loew and Mordecai Maisel – enjoyed influence in Rudolf II's court; Charles VI recognized the community's autonomy in 1716; his descendant Joseph II ended many discriminatory measures; and, in the late 19th century, Jews were active in the National Revival. But anti-Semitism still lurked. In 1899, Leopold Hilsner was accused of ritual murder; his counsel was Tomáš Garrigue Masaryk, future president of independent Czechoslovakia. Although the interwar years were a golden age for Czech Jews, among them Franz Kafka (see p44), the 1938 Munich Agreement gave Hitler possession of Czech lands, and the Jews' freedom was restricted to a ghetto, before being deported to concentration camps. Synagogues were turned into archives for looted Jewish artifacts. Hitler reportedly even planned to create a museum of an extinct race in Josefov. By the end of the war nearly 80,000 Bohemian and Moravian Jews had died in the Holocaust.

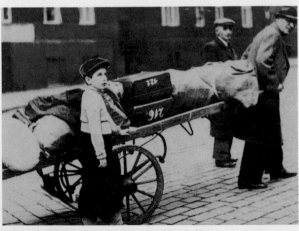

Father and son moving their belongings to the "ghetto" of Terezín

ᴛᴏᴘ10 National Gallery

Surrounded by the decorative Art Nouveau buildings of Holešovice, the austere Veletržní Palace is a daring work of art in itself. It was the first official Functionalist building in Europe, and even Le Corbusier was impressed by the eight-storey edifice when he visited Prague in 1928. After years as a trade fair complex, plans to turn the building into the home of the National Gallery's modern art collection were launched in 1979. Alongside prominent Czech contributions to modern art is a rich array of international masters from the 19th, 20th and 21st centuries.

Veletržní Palace façade

🍵 The café on the ground floor also doubles as an Internet café.

🕐 The first floor houses short-term exhibits. Check the weekly galleries listings of the Prague Post for details *(see p128)*.

Dukelských hrdinů 47, Holešovice
- Map B5
- 222 321459
- www.ngprague.cz
- Open 10am–6pm Tue–Sun
- Dis. access
- Adm varies according to exhibitions

Top 10 Paintings

1. House in Aix-en-Provence
2. Bonjour, Monsieur Gauguin
3. Rider Jaguar Attacking a Horseman
4. Green Wheat
5. St John the Baptist
6. Head of a Young Girl
7. At the Moulin Rouge
8. Myself, Self Portrait
9. Self Portrait
10. Anxiety

Entrance

House in Aix-en-Provence

The National Gallery's impressive collection of French art was begun in 1923, when Czech president Tomáš Masaryk helped found a small collection. This bright landscape *(above)* by Paul Cézanne was one of those original 25 pieces.

Bonjour, Monsieur Gauguin

Paul Gaugín's simple, flat self-portrait *(right)* was originally painted as a decoration for the lower panel of a dining-room door for a house in Brittany. The much-admired 19th-century French artist made this enlarged copy in 1889.

For details of other National Gallery sites in Prague **See p36**

3 Rider Jaguar Attacking a Horseman

Delacroix often visited zoos to study predatory animals whose movement inspired him. This small canvas from 1853 *(right)* is a fine example of such research, and is striking for its interaction of colour and motion.

5 St John the Baptist

Auguste Rodin's 1878 sculpture *(below)* is a study of spiral motion, from the tension of the firmly anchored feet, to the rotating trunk, to the head turned away from the dominant gesture of the right hand.

8 Myself, Self Portrait

With elements of modern civilization in the background Henri Rousseau's self portrait depicts the artist as a self-assured personality.

9 Self Portrait

One of 14 Picassos donated by former National Museum director Vincenc Kramář in 1960, the almond-shaped eyes and triangular nose testify to the influence of Iberian art and sculpture.

10 Anxiety

Otto Gutfreund paved the way for modern Czech sculpture. This bronze *(above)* captures the apprehension of man in the early 20th century.

Functionalism

Plans for a trade fair complex began in 1924. A design competition selected the work of architects Oldřich Týl and Josef Fuchs. Only the existing Veletržní Palace was completed; other planned buildings never materialized due to a lack of funding. Veletržní Palace opened in 1928 on the Republic's 10th anniversary. It was badly damaged by fire in 1974 and reopened to the public in 1995.

4 Green Wheat

Van Gogh's encounter with Impressionism was a decisive moment. Charmed by the countryside of southern France, he began to create bright canvases such as this landscape *(below)*.

6 Head of a Young Girl

Created in 1926, Henri Laurens' sculpture is a synthesis of Cubism and the Classical ideal of form and beauty. The National Gallery added Laurens' bronze to its collection in 1935.

7 At the Moulin Rouge

Toulouse-Lautrec thrived on depictions of Paris nightlife such as this oil tempura on cardboard. One of the dancing women is his muse, Jane Avril. Oscar Wilde is one of the figures in the background.

St Agnes's Convent

The 13th-century Convent of St Agnes of Bohemia (Klášter sv. Anežky) is an impressive Gothic building, closely tied to Czech statehood. Daughter of Přemysl Otakar I, Princess Agnes chose a spiritual life and founded a convent here in 1234 for the Poor Clares, an order of nuns associated with the Order of St Francis. But it was Agnes's diplomatic skills and work in establishing the convent which raised Bohemia in the eyes of Rome, as much as any courtly efforts to do the same. Restored in the 1960s to its original splendour, the convent is now used by the National Gallery to exhibit its collection of medieval and early Renaissance art.

Convent façade

With the exception of short-term exhibitions, the ground floor of the convent building is empty, but frequent chamber music concerts give visitors the opportunity to appreciate the pure Gothic spaces.

- U Milosrdných 17
- Map M1
- 224 810628
- www.ngprague.cz
- Open 10am–6pm Tue–Sun
- Dis. access
- Adm Kč150

Top 10 Works of Art

1. Strakonice Madonna
2. Zbraslav Madonna
3. Vyšší Brod Altarpiece
4. Works of Master Theodoricus
5. Třeboň Altarpiece
6. Capuchin Cycle
7. Velhartice Altarpiece
8. Martyrdom of St Florian
9. Puchner Altarpiece
10. Apocalypse Cycle

1 Strakonice Madonna

This larger-than-life, 700-year-old statue *(below)* of the Virgin and Child is the Czech National Gallery's most prized possession. The gestures of the Madonna are strikingly rigid, and evoke the Classical French sculpture found in places such as Reims Cathedral.

2 Zbraslav Madonna

Bohemia's most celebrated Marian painting is evocative of Byzantine icons in its style. The ring on the Madonna's left-hand finger symbolizes the Church through the mystical marriage between Christ and the Virgin Mary. The work has been moved to St Agnes's Convent from a Cistercian monastery where the majority of the Přemyslid kings were laid to rest.

3 Vyšší Brod Altarpiece

The 14th-century cycle begins with the *Annunciation*, then proceeds through the *Adoration of the Magi (below)* to *Pentecost (right)*. The creator of these beautiful panels is unknown.

Floorplan of St Agnes' Convent

Entrance

6 Capuchin Cycle

The origin of these 14 panels is unknown. The Virgin Mary is flanked by St Peter on the left and Christ on the right.

9 Puchner Altarpiece

St Agnes gave up a life at court to pursue a spiritual vocation. She is typically depicted nursing the sick on this 15th-century altarpiece.

10 Apocalypse Cycle

Although he's considered the foremost German Renaissance artist, Albrecht Dürer is probably best known for woodcuts such as this series of 15 from 1498 *(below)*, which retain a strong Gothic flavour.

7 Velhartice Altarpiece

Originating in south Bohemia around 1500, this is a rare example of a completely preserved altar *(above)*. Beneath the Madonna, cherubs hold the vera icon.

8 Martyrdom of St Florian

Albrecht Altdorfer created this painting as part of a multipanel altar featuring scenes from the legend of St Florian. Other pieces from the series are in Florence.

4 Works of Master Theodoricus

Parts of an altar set on loan from Karlštejn Castle, are *St Luke*, *St Charlemagne*, *St Catherine*, *St Matthew*, *St Ambrose* and *St Gregory*.

5 Třeboň Altarpiece

Only three of the five double-sided panels of the 14th-century Třebon Altarpiece *(right)* have survived to the present day.

St Agnes

St Agnes of Bohemia was a powerful figure in medieval politics. Pope Gregory IX granted special privileges to her convent and his successor Innocent IV sent priceless relics to be housed there. Agnes died in 1282, but her influence on Czech statehood was felt centuries later when, in 1989, Pope John Paul II canonized her; five days later, the Velvet Revolution began (see p35).

TOP 10 Wenceslas Square

This former medieval horse market began to be redeveloped in the 19th century, fast becoming the commercial hub of Prague – in 1848 it was renamed Wenceslas Square, in honour of Bohemia's patron saint. The majority of the buildings seen today date from the early 20th century, and their beautiful Art Nouveau façades illustrate the embracing of this style by Czech architects of the time. Often the scene of historic events, the most recent was in 1989, when crowds gathered to celebrate the end of Communism (see p35).

St Wenceslas Statue and the National Museum

Top 10 Sights

1. National Museum
2. St Wenceslas Statue
3. Communist Memorial
4. Palác Lucerna
5. Palác Koruna
6. Hotel Evropa
7. Svobodné slovo Balcony
8. Franciscan Gardens
9. Church of Our Lady of the Snows
10. St Wenceslas

○ Enjoy the faded glory of the Hotel Evropa over a coffee in its charming café.

○ Owing to the high volume of tourists, Wenceslas Square is home to many pickpockets. Be especially wary at the square's north end.

• Map N5

National Museum
Invading Warsaw Pact troops shelled the Neo-Renaissance building in 1968, assuming it was the Czechoslovak Parliament. The small entry fee is worth it, if only to see the museum's marble stairway *(above)* and pantheon of Czech cultural figures *(see p110)*.

OBĚTEM

St Wenceslas Statue
The Přemyslid prince sits astride a horse flanked by other Czech patrons *(below)* in Josef Myslbek's 1912 sculpture. The area "under the tail" is a traditional meeting place.

3 Communist Memorial
In front of St Wenceslas is a memorial to the victims of Communism *(below)*, such as two men who died in protest against the Warsaw Pact invasion in 1968.

6 Hotel Evropa
It's gone to seed over the years, but the Art Nouveau building at No. 25 *(below)* preserves its original façade and some original decor *(see p78)*.

7 Svobodné slovo Balcony
During the Velvet Revolution *(see p35)*, Václav Havel addressed pro-democracy demonstrators from the balcony of the *Svobodné slovo* newspaper building. When the deposed Alexander Dubček joined him, the crowds knew that Communism was over.

8 Franciscan Gardens
A stone's throw from the bustle of Wenceslas Square, these former monastery gardens provide much-needed peace from downtown.

Plan of Wenceslas Square

9 Church of Our Lady of the Snows
Founded by Charles IV upon his coronation in 1347, this lovely church *(below)* was to have been more than 100 m (330 ft) long, but it was never completed.

10 St Wenceslas
Hanging in the central passage of the Palác Lucerna is David Černý's take on the Czech patron saint. Vandals repeatedly remove the horse's tongue.

4 Palác Lucerna
President Václav Havel's grandfather designed and built this immense building on the square's western flank. It is now home to an art gallery, cinema, cafés, shops and a ballroom.

5 Palác Koruna
Built in "Geometric Modernist"style in 1912, this "palace" *(right)* became home to Turkish-style baths. Sadly, in 1997, it was taken over by a less romantic branch of Dunkin' Donuts.

Historic Demonstrations
Wenceslas Square saw its first demonstration in 1419 when Catholic reformer Jan Želivský led a procession to St Stephen's Church. On 28 October 1918 the area witnessed Czechoslovak independence. In 1969, Jan Palach set himself on fire here to protest against the Soviet occupation. It is still the scene of protests and victories today.

TOP 10 Petřín Hill

Covered with forests, orchards and strolling lovers, Petřín Hill creates a soft counterpoint to the spires of Hradčany on the Vltava's left bank. Rising more than 300 m (1,000 ft) above sea level, the area began life as a vineyard in the 15th century, but has been a public park since 1825. Early chronicles say it was the site of pagan rituals to the god Perun, and believers still practise ancient rites here on 1 May each year. Above all, however, it is the perfect escape when the city crowds become too much to bear.

Strahov Stadium
It may be ugly, but Strahov Stadium *(above)* is the largest arena of its kind in the world. It was built for Sokol, a physical culture organisation, and used for gymnastic rallies. Today it is a rock concert venue.

Strahov Monastery façade

Nebozízek restaurant (Petřínské sady 411) offers spectacular views of Prague from its window seats.

• Map C4
• Strahov Monastery: Open 9am–noon, 1pm–5pm daily, Adm
• Strahov Stadium: Closed to the public
• Observation Tower: Open 10am–5pm daily in winter Sat, Sun & hols only, (to 10pm in summer), Adm
• Mirror Maze: Open Apr–Aug: 10am–7pm daily, Sep–Oct: 10am–6pm daily, Nov–Mar: 10am–5pm Sat, Sun & hols, Dis. access, Adm
• Church of St Michael: Closed to the public
• Church of St Lawrence: Closed to the public • Funicular: Open 9am–11:20pm daily, Adm

Top 10 Features

1. Observation Tower
2. Strahov Stadium
3. Strahov Monastery
4. Mirror Maze
5. Hunger Wall
6. Karel Hynech Mácha Statue
7. Church of St Michael
8. Rose Gardens
9. Church of St Lawrence
10. Funicular

Observation Tower
Modelled after the Eiffel Tower in Paris, Petřín Hill's *Eiffelovka* stands only one-quarter as high as its inspiration, at 63.5 m (210 ft). It was created for the Jubilee Exposition of 1891. A climb of 299 stairs leads to the viewing platform.

Strahov Monastery
Founded in 1140, Strahov houses the nation's oldest books in the National Literature Museum while still functioning as a monastery. The Theological Hall, with its frescoes and statue of St John *(above)*, is a must-see.

For more parks and gardens in Prague **See pp40–41**

Mirror Maze
After laughing at the distorting mirrors in the labyrinth, take in a bit of history with a diorama depicting the final battle of the Thirty Years' War on Charles Bridge *(below)*.

Karel Hynech Mácha Statue
Mácha is a national poet, best loved for his Romantic poem "May". On 1 May, young lovers lay flowers at his statue's feet *(above)*.

Rose Gardens
At the top of the hill, catch your breath in the extensive rose gardens. Outside the nearby observatory is a memorial to Czech airmen who served during World War II.

Church of St Lawrence
The Stations of the Cross, created between 1834 and 1838, lead to the onion-domed Church of St Lawrence. Built on a pagan shrine in the 10th century, it was rebuilt in Baroque style in the 18th century.

Funicular
If you want to save your breath, do as visitors have done since 1891 and take the funicular railway to the top of the hill and walk down. The cable car offers outstanding views of the castle to the north.

Hunger Wall
The 14th-century wall *(below)* was originally part of the city's southern fortifications. Charles IV is said to have ordered its construction as a public works project to feed the poor during a famine.

Church of St Michael
No longer used for services, this lovely wooden church *(above)* was moved to Prague when the Ukraine valley it stood in was flooded by a dammed river.

Strahov Monastery Exhibits

Since its founding in the 12th century, Strahov Monastery has suffered fires, pillaging armies and totalitarian regimes. Josef II dissolved most local monasteries in 1783, but spared Strahov on the condition that the monks conduct research at their library. The majority of the research at the National Literature Museum today involves preserving the paper from being devoured by acidity. On display in the Theological and Philosophical Halls are old books, ornate gospels, miniature Bibles as well as a picture gallery.

Left **Charles IV** Right **Encampment of Matthias, Rudolph II's brother, 1608**

TOP 10 Moments in History

1 Wenceslas Assassinated
The "Good King" (actually a prince) was the second Christian ruler of Czech lands, succeeding his grandfather Bořivoj. Wenceslas solidified ties with Rome and with German merchants. Murdered by his brother in 935, he was later canonized.

2 Charles IV Becomes Holy Roman Emperor
Grandson of an emperor and son of a Přemyslid princess, Charles could hardly help rising to both the Roman and Bohemian thrones in 1333. Prague became the seat of imperial power under his reign, as well as an archbishopric and the home of central Europe's first university.

3 Hussite Wars
After the Church Council at Constance burned Catholic reformer Jan Hus at the stake in 1415 *(see p15)*, his followers literally beat their ploughshares into swords and rebelled against both church and crown. The resulting animosity between Protestant Czechs and German Catholics would rage for centuries.

4 Reign of Rudolph II
The melancholy emperor (1576–1611) was not much good as a statesman and was under threat from his ambitious brother, Matthias, but he was a liberal benefactor of the arts and sciences. Among his achievements were the support of Johannes Kepler's studies of planetary motion. He also promoted religious freedom.

5 Battle of White Mountain
The Protestant nobility and the emperor continued to provoke each other until hostilities broke into open war. Imperial forces devastated the Czechs in the first battle of the Thirty Years' War in 1620. Czech lands were re-Catholicized, but resentment against Vienna and Rome continued to smoulder.

6 Independence
While World War I raged, National Revival leaders such as Tomáš Masaryk turned to the United States for support for an independent Czechoslovakia. As the war drew to a close in 1918, the republic of Czechoslovakia was born.

Battle of White Mountain

7 World War II
The First Republic had barely stretched its legs when the Munich Agreement of 1938 gave Czech lands to Nazi Germany. Nearly 80,000 Czechs died in the Holocaust *(see p25)*. After the war, the nation exacted revenge by expelling its German citizens.

Nazi parade, Wenceslas Square, 1939

8 Rise of Communism
Grateful to the Red Army for liberating Prague in 1945, Czechoslovakia gave Soviet Communism the benefit of the doubt in the February 1948 elections.

9 Prague Spring
In 1968 First Secretary Alexandr Dubček introduced economic and social reforms that did not sit well with Moscow. Warsaw-Pact tanks rolled through Prague streets killing more than 100 protestors.

10 Velvet Revolution
After 10 days of mass protests in 1989, the Communist government bowed to the population's indignation. Czechs proudly recall that not a window was broken during the revolt.

Velvet Revolution celebrations

Top 10 Historical Figures

1 St Agnes
St Agnes (1211–82), devout sister of Wenceslas I, built a convent for the order of the Poor Clares (the female counterpart of the Franciscans).

2 St John of Nepomuk
Wenceslas IV arrested Nepomuk (1340–93) over the election of an abbot and threw his body from Charles Bridge.

3 Jan Hus
Hus (1370–1415) preached against Church corruption and was burned as a heretic.

4 Mordecai Maisel
The Jewish mayor (1528–1601) was one of the richest men in Europe *(see p22)*.

5 Tycho de Brahe
Astronomer at Rudolph's court, Brahe (1546–1601) suffered a burst bladder when he refused to leave the emperor's side at a banquet.

6 Edward Kelley and John Dee
The English charlatans gained Rudolph II's trust by converting lead into gold, but were more interested in necromancy.

7 Johannes Kepler
The German astronomer (1571–1630) pioneered studies of planetary motion.

8 Albrecht von Wallenstein
Leader of the Catholics during the Thirty Years' War, Wallenstein (1581–1634) built a vast palace in Prague *(see p86)*.

9 Franz Kafka
Prague's best-known author (1883–1924) was largely unpublished in his lifetime *(see p44)*.

10 Emil Zátopek
"The Locomotive" (1922–2000) won three long-distance gold medals at the 1952 Olympic Games.

Flooding in August 2002 caused a great deal of damage to many historic landmarks in Prague.

Left **National Gallery** Right **Prague Municipal Gallery**

TOP 10 Museums and Galleries

1 National Gallery

The National Gallery's extensive art collection is spread throughout the city in six locations. Kinský Palace holds the prints and drawings collection; St George's Convent the Mannerist and Baroque art *(see p9)*; St Agnes's Convent *(see pp28–9)*, medieval art; Sternberg Palace, the Old Masters; Veletržní Palace, the modern and contemporary collections *(see pp26–7)*; and Zbraslav Chateau, the collection of Asian art. ⊗ *Kinský; Palace: Staroměstské náměstí 12, Map M3, Open 10am–6pm Tue–Sun, Adm • Sternberg Palace: Hradčanské náměstí 15, Map B2, Open 10am–6pm Tue–Sun, Adm*

2 National Museum

The National Museum's collections are also spread throughout the country, but the flagship site is the historical and

National Museum

Statue of Music, Rudolfinum

natural history collections housed in the eponymous building at the top of Wenceslas Square *(see p110)*.

3 Rudolfinum

The "House of Artists" hosts a wide range of temporary exhibitions, each running several months. If you're at all a fan of contemporary art, it's always worth a visit, whatever aspect they are covering at the time. ⊗ *Alšovo nábřeží 12 • Map K2 • Open 10am–6pm Tue–Sun • Dis. access • Adm*

4 House of the Black Madonna

One of the finest Cubist buildings in Europe, the Black Madonna houses a permanent exhibition of Czech Cubism, as well as other Czech and international art dating from the first half of the 20th century. ⊗ *Celetná 34 • Map M4 • 224 211 746 • Open 10am–6pm Tue–Sun • Dis. access • Adm*

Prague Municipal Gallery

The city's finest 20th-century Czech art collection is on display at the House of the Golden Ring, while the House at the Stone Bell and Old Town Hall (see pp16–17) are used for temporary exhibitions. ⊗ House at the Golden Ring: Týnská 6, Map M3, Open 10am–6pm Tue–Sun, Adm • House at the Stone Bell: Staroměstské náměstí 13, Map M3, Open 10am–6pm Tue–Sun, Adm • www.ghmp.cz

Museum of Communism

Although there is a slightly kitsch element to the displays here, this new museum hopes to enable visitors to "experience" first hand 40 years of life under the Communist regime. Some critics assailed the entrepreneurs behind the show for not getting the approval of totalitarian experts, but it is nevertheless proving to be one of the city's more popular modern museums. ⊗ Na Příkopě 10 • Map N5 • Open 9am–9pm daily • Adm

House of the Black Madonna

Carved chest, Museum of Decorative Arts

Jewish Museum

The museum's collection of Judaic art is perhaps the world's largest, while other exhibits present the lives and history of Jews in Bohemia and Moravia. The collection is spread out around the synagogues of Josefov (see pp98–101).

Museum of Decorative Arts

The museum has recently spiced up its collection of crystal, porcelain and woodcarving with exhibitions of Czech fashion and other shows. ⊗ 17. listopadu 2 • Map L2 • Open 10am–6pm Wed–Sun, until 7pm Tue • Adm

National Technical Museum

The ultimate how-things-work museum, with exhibitions on mining, telecommunications and transport. Get a guide to show you the coal mine in the basement. ⊗ Kostelní 42 • Map M3 • Open 9am–5pm Tue–Fri, 10am–6pm Sat–Sun • Adm

Municipal Transport Museum

A celebration of more than 100 years of Prague's transport systems, from horse-drawn carriages to the metro. ⊗ Patočkova 4 • Map A1 • Open Apr–Nov: 9am–5pm Sat–Sun • Adm

Left **Holocaust wall, Pinkas Synagogue** Right **Monument, Cathedral of Sts Cyril and Methodius**

Places of Worship

1 St Vitus's Cathedral

The current building, looming over the castle complex with majesty, is a combination of architectural styles and took more than 500 years to complete. In days of old the cathedral was the setting of spectacular Bohemian coronations by Prague's archbishops. It's also the final resting place of the saints Wenceslas, John of Nepomuk and scores of other Czech worthies *(see pp12–13)*.

2 Old-New Synagogue

Prague's Orthodox Jewish community still holds services in this 700-year-old synagogue – the oldest in Europe. The building's curious name may come from the Hebrew *Al-Tenai*, meaning "with reservation". Legend has it that its stones will eventually have to be returned to Jerusalem, from whence they came *(see pp24–5)*.

Virgin Mary statue, Loreto

Madonna, Church of Our Lady Before Týn

3 Loreto

At the heart of this elaborate shrine to the Virgin Mary is the Santa Casa – a reproduction of the house where Mary received the Angel Gabriel. The Loreto treasury holds scores of priceless monstrances as well as other religious artifacts *(see pp20–21)*.

4 Church of Our Lady Before Týn

The Gothic towers of Týn loom over Old Town Square's houses. During the Counter-Reformation, the Jesuits melted down the gold Hussite chalice that stood between the towers and recast it as the Madonna seen today *(see p14)*. ◈ Staroměstské náměstí 14 • Map M3 • Open 10am–1pm, 3–5pm Tue–Sun • Dis. access • Free

5 Church of our Lady Victorious

This Baroque church contains the famed statue of the Infant Jesus of Prague. The wax baby doll is credited with miraculous powers. The resident Order of English Virgins look after the little man and change his clothes *(see p83)*.

Moorish decoration, Spanish Synagogue

Jewish Cemetery, as an emotive memorial *(see p25)*. The women's gallery was added in the 18th century *(see p101)*.

Church of St James
The Baroque façade is awash with cherubim and scenes from the lives of saints Francis of Assisi, James and Antony of Padua. It's an active house of worship, so gaze respectfully at the mummified arm hanging above the door inside *(see p74)*.

Church of St Nicholas
The Malá Strana church's cartoon-like clock tower and dome upstage its namesake across the river. The splendid Baroque sanctuary was meant to impress Catholic sceptics of the might of Rome *(see p82)*.

Spanish Synagogue
The present Moorish building with its opulent interior replaced Prague's oldest synagogue after the latter was razed in 1867. The Conservative Jewish community holds services here. It also houses Jewish Museum exhibits, offices and reference center *(see p101)*.

Pinkas Synagogue
The names of approximately 80,000 Czech victims of the Holocaust cover the walls of this house adjacent to the Old

Cathedral of Sts Cyril and Methodius
Nazi *Reichsprotektor* Reinhard "The Hangman" Heydrich's assassins *(see p106)* took refuge in this Eastern Orthodox Cathedral's crypt. The Gestapo executed the bishop who sheltered them.
Ⓢ Resslova 9 • Map E5 • Crypt: open May–Sep: 10am–5pm Tue–Sun; Oct–Apr: 10am–4pm Tue–Sun • Adm

Cathedral of Sts Cyril and Methodius

Left **Funicular, Petřín Hill** Right **Kampa Island**

TOP 10 Parks and Gardens

1 Petřín Hill
The views from here are so beautiful that susceptible romantics have been known to spontaneously kiss passers-by, including the monks from Strahov monastery. Best in spring when the orchards are in bloom *(see pp32–3)*.

Stromovka

2 Vyšehrad
Far enough from the centre to be largely tourist-free, Vyšehrad is the perfect place to be alone with your thoughts. Sights include the Neo-Gothic Church of Sts Peter and Paul, the graves of Dvořák and Smetana and reconstructed fortifications. There's very little shelter from inclement weather *(see p121)*.

3 Wallenstein Garden
General Albrecht von Wallenstein razed two dozen houses to make way for his expansive "backyard". Among the garden's stranger elements is the grotesquery on the southern wall, with stalactites imitating a limestone cave. The cries you hear all around you are the resident peacocks *(see p83)*.

4 Kampa Island
Malá Strana residents love to sunbathe, sip wine and play frisbee on the island green of the Little Quarter in summer. However, they also like to smoke marijuana, beat drums well into the night and use the grass for a public dog toilet, so watch your step *(see p82)*.

Wallenstein Garden

Vojanovy Sady
Prague's oldest garden was founded in the 13th century. It is home to peacocks, fruit trees and a heart-melting array of flowers *(see p83)*.

Stromovka
Otakar II established the royal hunting park here in 1266. A public garden since 1804, its ponds are ideal for ice-skating in winter and duck-feeding in summer. Its meandering paths offer easy strolling *(see p116)*.

Franciscan Garden
Stop here after pounding the Wenceslas Square pavement and join the pensioners and office workers at lunch, quietly filling the benches behind the Church of Our Lady of the Snows *(see p105)*.

Prague Castle Royal Gardens
These formal gardens were laid out by Ferdinand I in the 16th century. After mulling over the Belvedere summer palace and the Communist-revised frescoes on the Ball-Game Hall, slip down to the Stag Moat *(see pp8–11)*.

Střelecký Island
Lose yourself watching the Vltava rush past. Early risers can watch the sunrise strike the castle. In summer there's a popular outdoor cinema and live-music stage here. *Map D4*

Castle Terraces
The spectacular views of Malá Strana from this series of gardens descending from Prague Castle can't fail to inspire. This really is the best way to conclude a day of sightseeing at Hradčany *(see pp8–11)*.

Castle Terraces

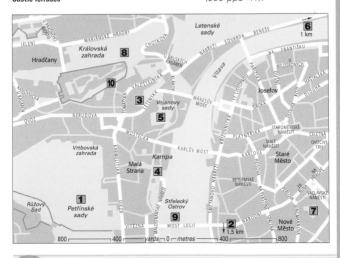

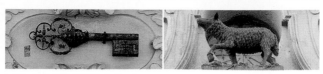

Left **The Golden Key** Right **The Red Lamb**

🔟 House Signs

1 The White Swan

Prague houses weren't given identifying numbers until 1770. Empress Maria Theresa was a great one for bringing the famed Habsburg trait of orderliness from Vienna to the banks of the Vltava. Before that, homes were known and located by a charming but confusing system of allegorical symbols. Although you can still find such emblematic addresses throughout the older parts of the city, Nerudova street in Malá Strana (see p81) has the highest concentration of house signs in the city. Originally many of them had alchemical significance, although today much of their meaning has been lost. The White Swan is one of these, and probably originated as a golden goose (not to be confused with the downtown department store of the same name, Bílá Labut'). ◈ Nerudova 49

2 The Two Suns

This house was the birthplace of the much-loved Czech poet and author Jan Neruda (1834–91), after whom the street is named. Traditionally this was the writers' and artists' area of Prague, and Neruda conveyed the Bohemian atmosphere of Malá Strana in his work. The connection continues today with the quarter's many small art galleries and craft shops. ◈ Nerudova 47

3 The Golden Key

Castle goldsmiths, such as the ones who worked at this house in the 17th century, paid fees to the city, unlike their colleagues who lived in the castle's Golden Lane (see p9). As such, they were entitled to advertise their wares, as preserved today in this building's façade. ◈ Nerudova 27

4 The Red Lamb

One of the street's more unlikely symbols, the scarlet sheep adorning this façade has an alchemical significance so arcane, not even the current house owner can explain it. Not that it matters – it remains in place as one of the city's many charming idiosyncrasies. ◈ Nerudova 11

The Two Suns

Apart from studying its beautiful house signs, Nerudova is a convenient route from the Old Town to Prague Castle.

St Wenceslas's Horse

in some quarters – are more interested in the meditative aspects of the art, however. ◈ *Nerudova 28*

8 The Three Fiddles
They say a demonic trio screeches on their instruments here on moonlit nights. The house was home to a family of violin-makers in the early 18th century, and the sign advertised their trade. Like many of the other buildings on this street, it is now home to a restaurant. ◈ *Nerudova 12*

9 The Devil
Lucifer pops up as a cuddly character on houses all over town and in local legend, more a folksy trickster than a sinister prince of darkness. Here, he'll tempt you to dine at a not completely infernal restaurant. ◈ *Nerudova 4*

10 The Green Lobster
Who knows what they were thinking when they hung the crustacean above their door. Probably trying to keep up with the neighbours at the Pendant Parsnip at No. 39. ◈ *Nerudova 43*

5 St Wenceslas's Horse
Clearly seen on the Old Town Square on the façade of Štorch House, this is a tribute both to the patron saint of Bohemia and the blacksmiths who shod horses bound for the castle. ◈ *Staroměstské náměstí*

6 The Three Lillies
Although their image no longer adorns the façade, the three flowers remain atop the house. The house also lends its name to a feverish tale of passion and thunderstorms by Jan Neruda. Many of the author's tales were set in houses such as this one. ◈ *Nerudova 15*

7 The Golden Wheel
Another alchemical symbol, the wheel represents a stage in the *magnum opus,* the process by which lead was purportedly turned into gold. Modern day alchemists – yes, they still exist

The Three Fiddles

Left **Karel Čapek** Centre **Franz Kafka and his fiancé** Right **Václav Havel**

🔟 Writers and Composers

1 Franz Kafka
Although he wrote in German and almost none of his work was published in his lifetime, Franz Kafka *is* Prague. Many of his disturbing novels seem to foresee the Communist years. His peripatetic wanderings across this city, brooding features and death by tuberculosis all add to the mystique.

2 Gustav Meyrink
Almost completely unknown outside Austria, Meyrink is nevertheless responsible for one of the city's most marketable notions: the Golem. He penned the story of the clay monster, that was supposedly locked up in the Old-New Synagogue, in 1914 and attributed its creation to the real Rabbi Loew *(see p52)*.

3 Karel Čapek
This Czech writer is best known for his science fiction and psychologically penetrating novels. With his 1921 play *R.U.R. (Rossum Universal Robots)* he gave the world a word for an automaton, based on a Czech word for "forced labour".

4 Jaroslav Hašek
A notorious joker and the author of the celebrated dig at the Austrian army, *The Adventures of the Good Soldier Švejk*, Hašek was also the creator of the satirical Party for Moderate Progress Within the Bounds of the Law.

5 Wolfgang Amadeus Mozart
Prague and Vienna continue to duel over the musical genius's legacy, with the Czechs always claiming that Mozart loved them better. The composer premiered his opera *Don Giovanni* in Prague's Estates Theatre *(see p65)* and Prague residents mourned spectacularly upon his death in 1791. Regular Mozart concerts are held in the city.

6 Bedřich Smetana
The composer wrote his opera *Libuše*, based on the legendary princess, for the reopening of Prague's National Theatre in 1883. Smetana vies with Antonín Dvořák for the title of best-loved Czech composer; the former's ode to beer in *The Bartered Bride* gives him a certain advantage.

Wolfgang Amadeus Mozart

Antonin Dvořák

Antonin Dvořák

Dvořák's works, such as his *Slavonic Dances*, regularly incorporate folk music. He composed his final symphony *From the New World* while he was director of the National Conservatory in New York City.

Bohumil Hrabal

The poetic author used to sit in the Old Town pub U Zlatého tygra *(see p60)*, taking down the stories he heard there. He died falling from his hospital-room window in 1997.

Václav Havel

The Czech president was known as a playwright before he became a civil rights activist protesting the Warsaw Pact invasion in 1968 *(see p35)*. His absurdist works and his fame helped draw international attention to his country's struggles.

Milan Kundera

Czechs have a love-hate relationship with their best-known contemporary author. Since his emigration to Canada, Kundera has had little to do with his native country, even writing his novels in French. His works convey a comic skepticism.

Top 10 Works of Art, Music and Literature

1 The Trial

The protagonist Joseph K. of Kafka's 1925 novel finds himself accused of a crime he did not commit.

2 The Castle

Kafka worked on this novel of social alienation while living in Prague Castle's Golden Lane *(see p9)*.

3 Adventures of the Good Soldier Švejk

Hašek was so effective in sending up the army and the Austro-Hungarian empire that Czechs still have a hard time taking authority seriously.

4 Slavonic Epic

Art Nouveau master Alfons Mucha celebrates the Czech mythic past in this artwork.

5 R.U.R.

Čapek's science-fiction play is a study of labour relations and social structures.

6 Grandmother

Author Božena Němcová based the narrator on her own grandmother, from whom she heard many of these stories.

7 Vltava

Smetana's *My Country* are six tone poems celebrating Bohemia. The second follows the river's course.

8 From the New World

With his 1893 ninth symphony, Dvořák incorporated the style of black folk songs.

9 Disturbing the Peace

Havel meditates on Communism and the values underlying Central Europe's pursuit of democracy.

10 The Unbearable Lightness of Being

Kundera's non-linear tale of love, politics and the betrayals inherent in both.

Left **Mission Impossible** Right **Kolya**

Film Locations

Amadeus

1 Amadeus

As a drunken Wolfgang Amadeus Mozart, Tom Hulce staggered through Malá Strana's narrow Thunovská alley in Miloš Forman's Academy Award-winning 1984 interpretation of Peter Shaffer's successful play. Prague was a well chosen location for the film, since Mozart's *Don Giovanni* debuted at the Estates Theatre *(see p65)*, and Praguers are intensely proud of the association.

2 The Unbearable Lightness of Being

Daniel Day Lewis and Juliette Binoche played an unhappily married couple living on Radnické schody during the 1968 Warsaw Pact invasion, in the 1988 film adaptation of Milan Kundera's dark novel about love, relationships and betrayal *(see p45)*.

3 Mission: Impossible

Cars explode on Kampa Island, restaurants explode on the Old Town Square. The opulent party in the thriller's opening scene takes place in the National Museum, in this 1996 sci-fi fantasy starring Tom Cruise.

4 Les Misérables

Jean Valjean, played by Liam Neeson, fled from the *gendarme* on Hradčanské náměstí through Prague sewers in the 1998 re-make of this classic tale. Neeson also fled from fans at Molly Malone's Irish pub.

5 The Shooter

In a chase scene, Dolph Lundgren leaps from a rooftop at Prague Castle and lands, miraculously, on the National Theatre; Prague audiences were unimpressed by this lack of authenticity in 1995.

Les Misérables

The Unbearable Lightness of Being

6 From Hell
The Hughes brothers turned Saská Alley near Charles Bridge and other Malá Strana locations into Jack the Ripper's foggy London in 2001. Off-screen, Johnny Depp retreated to the smoky depths of the Blue Light bar on Josefská.

7 Plunkett and Macleane
Jonny Lee Miller and Robert Carlyle blunderbuss their way up and down Thunovská. Locals were used as 18th-century extras for the 1999 production.

8 Kolya
In 1996 Jan Svěrák cast his father Zdeněk as the grumpy, philandering cellist who restores Olšanská cemetery tombstones in his free time. The five-year-old title character gets lost in Anděl metro station (see p49).

9 The Bourne Identity
Jindřišská and Panská near Wenceslas Square serve as Zurich in this 2002 film adaptation of Robert Ludlum's novel.

10 Dungeons and Dragons
Even with the special effects, Prague's skyline and Charles Bridge are easily recognizable in this sword-and-sorcery epic of 2000.

Top 10 Czech Filmmakers

1 Miloš Forman
The Academy Award-winning director of *One Flew Over the Cuckoo's Nest* (1975) returned to his homeland to film *Amadeus*.

2 Jan Svěrák
This young director is carrying Czech filmmaking into the 21st century with films such as *Kolya* (1996).

3 Jan and Eva Švankmajer
Director Jan creates films in which his wife Eva's Surrealist animated objects come to life.

4 Gene Deitch
Deitch was a little-known animator before he took a job producing films in Communist Czechoslovakia. He fell in love with the city and stayed.

5 Gustav Machatý
When a young Slovak actress took off her clothes in Machatý's *Ecstasy* (1932) it became the first film to feature nudity; the actress became Hedy Lamarr.

6 Petr Zelenka
This young turk focuses on oddballs in films such as *Loners* (2000).

7 Jiří Menzel
Menzel won the country's first Academy Award with *Closely Watched Trains*.

8 Výra Chytílová
The *grande dame* of Czech cinematography – her best film is *Daisies* (1966).

9 Karel Vachek
Vachek creates rambling documentaries which capture the absurdity of Czech politics.

10 Ivan Reitman
Reitman, now US-based, is best known for directing the hit *Ghostbusters*.

Left **Strahov Stadium** Right **Anděl Metro**

Communist Monuments

1 Žižkov TV Tower

The city's most hated building among Praguers was built in the 1970s, and was intended, according to rumour, to jam foreign radio signals or emit nefarious radiation. Despite its ugly, utilitarian design, however, the view of Prague's skyline from the top of the 100-m (330-ft) tower is spectacular on a clear day *(see p117)*.

2 Monument of National Liberation

After a failed attempt to embalm President Klement Gottwald after his death, the Communist government was forced to cremate their favoured leader. His ashes, as well as those of various other *apparatchiks*, were buried here atop Vítkov Hill, behind the giant statue of Jan Žižka. They were removed after the Velvet Revolution *(see p35)*, and in reparation, the National Museum hopes to create a monument to the victims of totalitarianism on the site.
◈ *Vítkov hill, Žižkov • Map B6 • Closed to the public*

3 Strahov Stadium

Prague Castle would fit inside this massive arena situated on Petřín Hill. The stadium was built for Sokol, an organisation that promoted physical culture. It was first used in 1926 to host traditional gymnastic rallies or *slets*. Today, the stadium is a popular music venue and local kids crowd in to see the likes of U2, Ozzy Osbourne and numerous other touring rock bands *(see p32)*.

4 Letná Plinth

Where sculptor David Černý's giant metronome now swings once stood a 14,000-ton statue of Joseph Stalin – the largest in the world – backed by a queue of admiring citizens, which was visible from all over the city. His successor Nikita Khrushchev had the statue destroyed by a series of dramatic dynamite explosions in 1962. Pop star Michael Jackson launched his 1996 World Tour in Prague, unwisely erecting a statue of himself on the spot.
◈ *Letenské sady, Letná • Map E1*

Sbratření

Czech Radio Building

Congress Centre
Communist Czechoslovakia's planners sought to decentralize Prague, building monoliths such as the former Palace of Culture anywhere but in the actual city centre. The post-Communist government has refurbished the interior in a bid to turn it into a major convention centre, but, as yet, they haven't managed to find a buyer *(see p121)*.

Anděl Metro
In the reconstruction of the Anděl Centre, developers removed an epic mosaic tribute to the friendship between Moscow and Prague, but from the metro platforms below, you can still see frieze tributes to Soviet cosmonauts. Even if you're not riding the metro, you will need a standard ticket to access the platform. ◈ *Map A6*

Sbratření
This bronze statue recalls the Red Army's liberation of Prague in 1945: a grateful resistance fighter greets a Soviet footsoldier with a bunch of lilac and a, presumably brotherly, kiss. It's one of the few pro-Soviet monuments still standing in Prague. ◈ *Vrchlického sady • Map G4*

Czech Radio Building
Warsaw-Pact tanks invaded the Czech capital in 1968 to put an end to Alexander Dubček's Prague Spring liberalization. Among those who paid for their resistance with their lives were Czech Radio journalists, who first broadcast the news that the nation was under attack. A plaque in front of the building honours their bravery. ◈ *Vinohradská 12, Vinohrady • Map B6 • Closed to the public*

RFE Building
From its construction in the 1970s until Czechoslovakia split into Czech and Slovak republics in 1993, this was the Federal Assembly building. If there are bored young soldiers guarding the entrance when you visit, it means Radio Free Europe is still broadcasting to Afghanistan. ◈ *Vinohradská 1, New Town • Map H5 • Closed to the public*

Museum of Communism
This museum seeks to help visitors experience totalitarianism first-hand through reproductions and genuine objects from the Communist era. The most chilling area is the reconstructed interrogation room. Although locals might not agree, the tour is more fun than it sounds *(see p37)*.

Museum of Communism

System

Left **Poster, Wax Museum Praha** Right **National Marionette Theatre**

Eccentric Prague

1 Museum of Torture Instruments

If you can't quite grasp how these grisly instruments work, the helpful illustrations should make their operation painfully clear. More than 60 implements of pain from all over Europe are on display, accompanied by explanations in several languages. Ⓢ *Křižovnické náměstí 1 • Map J4 • Open 10am–10pm daily (to 8pm in winter) • Adm*

2 Rock Therapy

Subtitled "a Small Story From the Great Time of the Beatles", this non-verbal show uses film projection, music, dance and puppetry to present "a loosely poetical black-theatrical production of the animated film *Yellow Submarine*". It is, if nothing else, a unique synthesis of various Czech theatre genres. Must be seen to be believed, whether you're a Beatles fan or not. Ⓢ *Animato Theater, Na Příkopě 10 • Map N5 • Adm*

3 Wax Museum Praha

Bohemia's great figures all come together in one happy community here, with lifelike waxwork representations of Franz Kafka, Rudolf II and The Good Soldier Švejk, making for a wonderful stroll through Czech history. The presence of Bill Clinton, Elton John, Tina Turner and other modern icons is a little more difficult to fathom. Ⓢ *Melantrichova 5 • Map L4 • Open 9am–8pm daily • Adm*

4 Marionette Don Giovanni

Mozart premiered his opera *Don Giovanni* at Prague's Estates Theatre in 1787. Of the two marionette homages to the city's favourite opera, the better production takes place at the National Marionette Theatre. The technique of the puppeteers is so masterful, you'll leave looking for strings attached to passers-by. A true Prague experience *(see p65)*.

5 Exhibition of Spiders and Scorpions

In case the torture museum wasn't enough to make your skin crawl, this creepy mini-zoo has more than 100 live little beasts for your amusement. Although the tiny monsters are not native to Bohemia, you'll be shaking out

Museum of Torture Instruments

Exhibition of Spiders and Scorpions

your bedsheets for the rest of your stay. ✆ Křižovnické náměstí 1 • Map J4 • Open 10am–10pm daily (to 8pm in winter) • Adm

Sex Machine Museum

An exhibition in a slightly different sense, this is one show definitely not for the kids. The museum traces the history of gratifying instruments from their origins to the modern day. While not entirely without cultural merit, the overall package is rather bizarre. There is, predictably, a gift shop. ✆ Melantrichova 18 • Map L4 • Open 10am–11pm daily • Adm

Křižík Fountain

Each summer evening, the fountain's 50 pumps, 3,000 water jets and more than 1,200 lights put on a dizzying display of hydro-mechanic choreography. The musical accompaniment ranges from classical to heavy metal to

Disney tunes. Recent productions have included live folk dance troupes and a melodrama based on James Bond plots (see p116). ✆ Výstaviště, Holešovice • Map B5

Marionette Marriage of Figaro

Mozart's comic opera adapts well to the grotesque puppets and the techniques of marionette theatre. It's high art and, despite the efforts of the expert puppeteers, the illusion is a bit hard to maintain, but patient opera fans will enjoy the novelty. ✆ Staroměstské náměstí 12 • Map M3

Marionette Orpheus et Euridice

Take an eternal tale of humanity's search for meaning in the cycle of life, death and rebirth, add a century of Czech marionette tradition and a fuzzy soundtrack, and mix well. Watching the bemused audience is almost as much fun as the action on stage. ✆ National Marionette Theatre: Žatecká 1 • Map L3

Operetta

The Czech love of operetta knows no limits, except perhaps the number of performers willing to take part in the latest rock opera at locations around town. It began with Romany and Juliette, proceeded to Dracula and is still going strong with a romping Monte Cristo. Check The Prague Post for performance times (see p128). ✆ Divadlo Broadway: Na Příkopě 31; Map N5 • Divadlo Ta Fantastika: Karlova 8; Map L4 • Hvdební Divadlo Karlín Křižíkova 10 • Map H2

Křižík Fountain

Left **The Golem** Centre **One-Armed Thief** Right **Emaus Monastery**

⟨TOP⟩10 Haunted Places

1 Ghost tour
Local resident Michal Fried dons a white cloak each night and leads visitors through an after-dark ramble around the Old Town in search of some of Prague's ghostly nightlife. To join the tour, look out for the ghoulish-looking man standing beneath the Old Town Hall's Astronomical Clock (see p16).

2 Turk in Ungelt
Among the merchants who lived in the Týn settlement behind the Church of Our Lady (see p14) was a Turkish immigrant. When his betrothed ran off and married another, he flew into a rage and chopped her head off. He is said to wander around the Ungelt courtyard carrying the decapitated head.

3 One-Armed Thief
Rumour has it that a thief sought to steal jewels from a statue of the Madonna in the Church of St James (see p74), but the stony Virgin seized him by the arm and local butchers had to cut him loose. According to some, he still haunts the church asking visitors to help him fetch his arm, which hangs from the wall inside.

4 The Golem
Rabbi Loew created his clay robot to help out around the house. When the creature raised a ruckus on the sabbath, Loew was forced to deactivate him and stashed him in the attic of the Old-New Synagogue (see p24).

5 The Iron Man
Believing his fiancée had been untrue, a knight called off his wedding. After she drowned herself in grief, he realized his mistake and hanged himself. Every 100 years he "appears" in Platnéřská Street, hoping to find a young woman to free him. His next appearance is due in 2009.

6 The Drowned Man
When the bicycle was all the rage in the late 19th century, young Bobeř Říma stole one and rode it into the river. If a soggy young fellow tries to sell you a bike near the Old Town end of Charles Bridge, just keep walking.

7 Emaus Devil
In an attempt to bedevil the monks at the Emaus Monastery, Satan took a job there as a cook and seasoned their food with pepper and other spices. To this day, Czech cuisine has few piquant flavours.

The Iron Man

Werewolf

8 Werewolf

Apparently, Rudolph II's gamekeeper became so enamoured of the wolves that roamed the castle's Stag Moat that he became one himself. Nowadays, he takes the form of a large dog and tends to chase cyclists, joggers and tourists when the whim takes him, so keep looking over your shoulder.

9 Drahomira

St Wenceslas's mother was, by all accounts, an unpleasant woman. She killed her mother-in-law and might have done in her son, too, but the gates of hell swallowed her up before she could act. She sometimes wheels through Loretánská náměstí in a fiery carriage.

10 The Mad Barber

When a local barber foresook his home and family after he became caught up in alchemical pursuits, his daughters ended up in a brothel and his wife killed herself. He is said to haunt the vicinity of Karlova and Liliova streets, hoping to return to his honest profession and make amends.

Top 10 False Stories

1 Czechs are Celts
Some Czechs claim that a Celtic tribe known as the Boii inhabited Bohemia, but their roots are Germanic and Slavic.

2 Vyšehrad Castle
Vyšehrad was the first seat of power, but its importance has been inflated by legend.

3 Alchemists Lived in Golden Lane
Alchemists tended to live on credit in houses in town.

4 Jan Nepomuk Died on Charles Bridge
Nepomuk was already dead when he was thrown over the side (see p19).

5 Jan Masaryk Committed Suicide
In 1948 the Foreign Minister was found dead in front of Černín Palace, having "fallen" from a window, according to the Communists.

6 There's Only One Bud
The town of České Budějovice (Budweis in German) was producing beer before the US brewer, but didn't register copyright on the name.

7 Czech Hippies Painted the John Lennon Wall
The image of Lennon was the post-Communist work of a Mexican art student (see p81).

8 Absinthe Will Make You Crazy
The amount of wormwood in the drink is negligible.

9 Marijuana is Legal
Czech law punishes anyone caught with "more than a small amount" of the drug.

10 Prague is the New Left Bank
After the Revolution, some wag proclaimed Prague "the Paris of the '90s", due to the number of free-loading expats.

Prague's Top 10

Left **Mirror Maze entrance** Right **Gargoyle, St Vitus's Cathedral**

Children's Attractions

Mirror Maze
The warped mirrors lining the walls here are great fun for making faces, pointing fingers at distended bellies and elongated bodies and giggling hysterically, whatever your age. For older children interested in a bit of gore and history combined, the battle-scene diorama is another of the many attractions on Petřín Hill *(see pp32–3)*.

Swan Feeding
Grab a bag of breadcrumbs and head to the riverbank. Střelecký Ostrov is an ideal spot to watch these graceful white birds dip their necks in the water to catch the morsels for children's delight. Take care that little feet don't go into the water and mud, however, and make sure that fingers don't inadvertently get snapped in the feeding frenzy. Good for all seasons. ◊ *Map D4*

Czech puppets

Puppet Shows
Puppetry is a long-standing Czech tradition, and late afternoon shows will keep kids entertained for up to an hour. There's enough action that younger folk usually don't mind not understanding the libretto or narration. Weekend presentations of well-known fairy tales at the National Marionette Theatre can fill up quickly, so book in advance *(see p65)*.

Gargoyle-Spotting
It's habit-forming. Give the little ones their first taste finding faces on St Vitus's Cathedral *(see pp12–13)* and they'll have their heads pointed upwards for days. In addition to gargoyles, train your kids to spot the innumerable statues, house signs *(see pp42–3)* and strange faces that adorn arches, cornices and gateways all over the city. Just take care that they don't get stiff necks or stumble on uneven pavement surfaces.

White Tower
This is an entertaining spot at Prague Castle. Here they can shoot a real crossbow, pick out their favourite suit of armour and imagine the grisly goings-on in the torture chamber. Little people will have no trouble negotiating the low, narrow passages, but adults might. ◊ *Zlatá ulička, Prague Castle • Map C2 • Open Apr–Oct: 9am–6pm, Nov–Mar: 9am–4pm • Adm*

Boat on the Vltava

Historic Tram No. 91

The old-fashioned streetcar runs a circuit around the city in about 30 minutes. A friendly conductor will take your Kč35 fare and you can hop on and off at any stop on the route, including Malostranská and Národní divadlo (see p65). Very handy when you can't face walking another step. For those who are planning ahead, the end station is Výstaviště, scene of more excitement. 🅢 Map B5 • Mar–Nov: noon–5:35pm Sat & Sun • www.dpp.cz

Výstaviště

In addition to Křižík Fountain, the Prague exhibition grounds are home to the Lunapark carnival: ferris wheels, rollercoasters and similar other rides will toss and turn the kids for hours, and, if they can still stomach it, there's even candy floss (cotton candy). The fun begins in March and carries on through the warmer summer months (see p116).

Boat Trips

While adults might enjoy the old-fashioned (and more romantic) rowboats, children prefer the splashing, pedalling action of the miniature paddleboats that travel up and down the Vltava. Numerous vendors rent boats and sell tickets in the vicinity of Charles Bridge (see pp18–19). Take all the usual precautions that no one goes overboard, accidentally or otherwise.

Black Light Theatre

There is an abundance of Black Light shows around the Old Town (see p65), but the best is at Divadlo Ta Fantastika. So long as the kids don't mind strange images suddenly popping out of the dark, the brilliant displays should keep them mesmerized. 🅢 Divadlo Ta Fantastika, Karlova 8 • Map K4

Křižík Fountain

First, bring a sweater. Second, don't sit too close to the water. Third, sit back and enjoy the show. The dancing water-and-light show's musical accompaniment varies from classical to pop to Disney tunes. The Prague Post (see p128) lists the programme in its weekly calendar (see p116).

Lunapark Carnival, Výstaviště

Left **Eduard Čapek** Right **Hračky**

Shops and Markets

1 Dr Stuart's Botanicus
Here you'll find oils and salts for that hot bath your travel-weary feet crave, as well as perfumes, candles, soaps and every natural health and beauty product you can imagine. Branches are scattered around town but the main one is off the Old Town Square (see p76).

2 Museum Shop
This is the shop for unique gifts and souvenirs for travellers with discerning tastes. Instead of another T-shirt, how about a scarf patterned after a window at St Vitus's Cathedral? There's also a wide selection of prints, fabrics, masks, books and trinkets, modelled on items in Prague's museums. ◉ Karlova 21 • Map L4

3 Havelský trh
The Old Town's largest outdoor market. Monday through Friday, the stalls in front of St Havel are crowded with produce as well as handicrafts and textiles. The greengrocers stay away at weekends, leaving more room for souvenirs. ◉ Havelský trh • Map M5

Art Deco

4 Art Deco
Enter this shop filled with antique furnishings, vintage clothing and one-of-a-kind knick-knacks and you'll feel you've stepped back into the First Republic. Outfit yourself in Jazz-Age style, right down to the spats and cigarette holder, or dress up your parlour with an Art Nouveau clock or cordial set. ◉ Michalská 21 • Map L5

5 Galerie u bílého jednorožce
Tucked in an 11th-century cellar under Týn Church, the Gallery at the White Unicorn specializes in hand-painted silk ties, scarves and throws, many with local motifs. Unique wood, leather and fabric gifts, too. Watch your step on the stairs. ◉ Staroměstské náměstí 15 • Map M3

6 Eduard Čapek
Prague's favourite junk shop. As the rest of the Old Town goes up-market, this little hole in the wall keeps up a lively trade in trinkets and gossip. Very little gets sold and it's hard to

Dr Stuart's Botanicus

 For tips on shopping in Prague See p132

understand how the shop stays in business, but if your decorating calls for rust and dust, this is your supplier.
🛇 Dlouhá 32 • Map M2

Dorotheum
Dorotheum offices throughout the world trace their roots back to the Vienna pawn-broking office, established by Emperor Josef I in 1707. A member of the Association of International Auctioneers, Dorotheum holds large auctions several times a year and maintains a large sales gallery of silverware, fine china, jewellery, art and other collectors' items.
🛇 Ovocný trh 2 • Map N4

Blue
Forget the traditional image of dust-collecting glass bowls and stemware. Blue's bold and quirky designs will brighten your living room, dining room or bathroom like no old-fashioned glass can. Plus, the prices are low enough that you won't hesitate to use your purchases every day. You can also pick up the requisite T-shirts, picture books and other gifts here if you wish (see p76).

Blue

Hračky
This small shop is crammed full with hundreds of charming toys. Traditional, hand-painted folk dolls, wind up toys, con-struction sets and model trains are just some of the goods on offer. Take advantage of the reasonable prices which are lower than elsewhere in Prague.
🛇 Loretánské náměstí 3 • Map A2

Erpet Bohemia Crystal
A one-stop shop for glass and jewellery. Erpet sells Bohemian lead crystal, garnet jewellery, enamel glass and chandeliers, as well as fine goods from the Moser, Goebel and Swarovski manufacturers. Shoppers can ponder the purchases they're about to make over coffee in the shop's comfortable lounge area.
🛇 Staroměstské náměstí 27 • Map M3

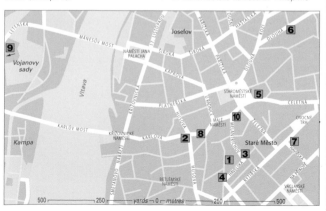

Left **Potato knedlíky with sauerkraut** Centre **Rohlíky** Right **Liver knedlíky in beef broth**

🔟 Prague Dishes

1 Guláš
Not quite as spicy as its Hungarian cousin, Czech goulash is essentially a rich beef stew minus the vegetables. Don't even think of ordering it without *knedlíky* dumplings on the side. Beef is the standard recipe of this staple dish, but you can sometimes find goulash using venison, chicken and even vegetarian variants.

2 Svíčková na smetaně
This is goulash's sweet cousin: slices of pot-roasted beef tenderloin are served in a carrot-sweetened cream sauce, topped with a dollop of whipped cream and cranberries. Apparently, this is one of President Václav Havel's favourite dishes. Like goulash, it's unthinkable to eat it without the dumplings to mop up the sauce.

3 Smažený sýr
Comparable to fried mozzarella sticks, this battered block of deep-fried mild cheese is usually served with French fries *(hranolky)* and a tangy tartare sauce. As with much of Czech cuisine, try not to think about the cholesterol.

4 Utopence
These pickled sausages, slightly sour, fatty and always piled high with pickled onions, are an ideal accompaniment to the local beer, as a lunchtime or early evening snack.

5 Knedlíky
These doughy dumplings are the side dish of choice for many gravy-laden Czech dishes. In addition to the savoury varieties, made with bread, potato or bacon *(špekové)*, *knedlíky* also come stuffed with fruit *(ovocné knedlíky)*, the most popular variety being plums *(švestkové)*.

6 Pivní sýr
"Beer cheese" is marinated in ale until semi-soft. It is best enjoyed spread on dark sourdough bread and sprinkled with chopped onions.

7 Syrečky
Also known as *olomoucké tvarůžky*, these small cheese rounds immediately announce themselves by their pungent aroma. Eat them as a snack or light lunch, accompanied by beer, bread and onions.

Svíčková na smetaně

Ovocné knedlíky

8 Vepřoknedlozelo

This name is the shortened version for *vepřová, knedlíky a zelí* – pork, dumplings and sauerkraut. Heavy on fat and low on flavour, this is true Czech soul food. Order it instead of goulash and you'll impress your waiter with how acclimatized you are, assuming you pronounce it right, of course.

9 Halušky

The Germans call these coarse little noodles *Spaetzel*. They're included in the Czech culinary canon as a nod to nearby Slovakia, from which they originate and with whom Bohemia has shared so much history. You can either order them *s zelím* (with sauerkraut) or *s bryndzou* (with a creamy, sharp cheese). The dish is a filling and cheap Eastern European alternative to pasta.

10 Rohlíky

The work-horse of the Prague diet, these ubiquitous banana-shaped bread rolls are served up to accompany the main meal at breakfast, lunch and dinner. Dip them in soft cheese or your dish's sauce, spread them with pâté or order them hot-dog style on nearly every street corner.

Top 10 Czech Beers

1 Staropramen

The home-town favourite has a light, fruity flavour. Brewed in the Smíchov district, its popularity owes as much to marketing as it does to local pride.

2 Pilsner Urquell

The best-known Czech beer on the international market comes from the town of Plzeň, 80 km (50 miles) southwest of Prague. It has a strong, hoppy flavour.

3 Krušovice

Rudolph II established the Krušovice brewery, which produces this sweet and somewhat flat beer. Try the syrupy dark *(tmavé)* variety.

4 Budvar

Brewed in the town of České Budějovice, the beer is no relation to the American Budweiser *(see p53)*.

5 Velkopopovický Kozel

This strong, smooth beer is well worth seeking out – some consider it the world's finest.

6 Velvet

This sophisticated stout, brewed by Staropramen, is catching on in Prague.

7 Gambrinus

In light and dark varieties, this is the best-selling beer in the country.

8 Bernard

This unpasteurized beer has a distinct, bitter-sweet flavour and a hoppy aroma.

9 Herold

Here's a twist: Americans brewing beer in Bohemia. The centuries-old recipe produces a caramel, malty brew.

10 Braník

Braník is made with real Vltava river water, giving it its distinct flavour.

Left **Pivovarský dům** Right **U Zlatého tygra**

TOP10 Bars and Kavárnas

Café Slavia

1 U Fleků
The city's oldest brewing pub, U Fleků is famous for its delicious, dark lager and somewhat more than modest prices. Despite what anyone tells you, the Becherovka shots are not complimentary and the rounds keep coming until you say "ne" five times. Very popular with busloads of tourists, and not without reason *(see p112)*.

2 Pivovarský dům
Excellent, rustic Czech fare served in a genteel setting. The house brewmaster is always concocting strange new flavours for his drinks, such as coffee lager or champagne ale. You can also watch the fermenting vats that will eventually become beer, if the process of brewing interests you. Ⓢ *Lipová 15 • Map F6 • 224 921256 • Dis. access •* **KK**

3 Café Slavia
Across from the National Theatre and on a busy river thoroughfare, Café Slavia with its 1930s Art Deco interior is a famous literary café. Enjoy a coffee and dessert at the end of the day or after a night at the theatre admiring the view of the riverside and Prague Castle. Ⓢ *Smetanovo nábřeží 2 • Map J6 • 224 239 604 •* **K**

4 U Zlatého tygra
This legendary pub, famed as the haunt of the late writer Bohumíl Hrabal *(see p45)*, serves the finest mug of Pilsner Urquell in the city. Regulars were non-plussed when President Václav Havel brought former US president Bill Clinton in for a cold glass, so don't expect them to take much interest in you. If you find a seat, it probably means one of the regulars has died. Ⓢ *Husova 17 • Map L4 • 222 221111 • No credit cards •* **K**

5 Tretter's
This is Prague's – and perhaps Europe's – best cocktail bar. It may look like a Jazz-Age time capsule, but Tretter's is actually a relative newcomer, and highly welcome at that. You'll find no bottle juggling, just

Tretter's

Kavárna *is the Czech name for a Prague coffeehouse.*

O' Che's

serious mixology, very dry martinis and, if you're lucky, a seat. Open until 3am. ⓥ *V Kolkovně 3* • Map L2 • 224 811165

Bugsy's
The kind of bar where you'll find well-heeled septugenarian gents with a girl on either arm. With top-notch drinks, sit at the bar for the best service but look smart as the under-dressed are turned away. ⓥ *Pařížská 10* • Map L2 • *224 810287* • www.bugsybar.com

Grand Café Orient
Designed during the Cubist movement in 1912, fans will love the building's architecture and be fascinated by the tower of cakes that greets them at the entrance. The café serves everything from tea, breakfast and lunch menus as well as wine and cocktails. ⓥ *Ovocný trh 19* • Map N4 • *224 224240* • **K**

Alcohol Bar
A straightforward approach to cocktails, as the name suggests. The superior circulation system, which is a novelty in Prague, filters the ubiquitous cigarette smoke from the atmosphere. DJs play classic rock and Motown tracks and the kitchen serves small plates of snacks for the peckish until 3am. ⓥ *Dušní 6* • Map L1 • *224 224 240* • *224 811744*

O'Che's
An improbable combination of Irish and Cuban themes actually works a treat, with Sunday roasts and Guinness on tap. When the football's on, expect the bar to be filled with a hooligan-free crowd of locals, tourists and expatriates. Unfortunately, the fun stops at midnight. ⓥ *Liliová 14* • Map K5 • *222 221178* • www.oches.com

Chateau Rouge
The bar next to the Church of St James *(see p74)* has lost some, but not all, of the seediness that characterized its previous incarnation, where the motto was "the customer is always wrong". Backpackers still chat to each other up over absinthe, however, and men in the street will offer you hashish on your way in. It may sound unappealing, but it's a true Prague experience. ⓥ *Jakubská 2* • Map N3 • *222 316328*

For a guide to price ranges See p79

Left **Alcron** Right **Kampa Park**

Restaurants

1 Kampa Park

Consistently rated Prague's best restaurant, chic Kampa Park has an unparalleled riverside location and an outstanding menu with influences from all over the world. Proprietor Nils Jebens also owns another restaurant at Nevudova Street *(see p89)*.

2 La Degustation (Bohême Bourgeoise)

One of the most intriguing dining experiences in Prague, with chefs offering a choice of three, seven-course taster menus that unfold over a three-hour period. Efficient staff and a classy location. ◈ *Haštalská 18 • Map N2 • 222 311234 • Dis. access •* **KKK**

3 Pravda

Around the corner from the Old-New Synagogue *(see pp24–5)* is where the other half dines on a multi-national menu before unwinding in the music bar downstairs. The window counters are ideal for people-watching. ◈ *Pařížská 17 • Map L2 • 222 326203 • Dis. access •* **KKKKK**

Pravda

V Zátiší

4 V Zátiší

Prague was introduced to fine dining at this small Bethlehem Square restaurant. The *dégustation* menu – a selection of tasters – brings out the kitchen's best and pairs it with select Moravian wines. The seafood is so good you'll forget you're in a landlocked country. ◈ *Liliová 1 • Map K5 • 222 221155 • Dis. access •* **KKKKK**

5 U Zlaté Studně

Dining atop the hotel of the same name *(see p138)*, guests "At the Golden Well" may think they've died and gone to heaven. The classic Continental cuisine matches the view – but only just. The dining room is tiny, so be sure to make a reservation. ◈ *U Zlaté Studně 4 • Map C2 • 257 533322 •* **KKKK**

6 Alcron

Seafood is the speciality at the Radisson's new restaurant, but the chef is happy to prepare almost any dish. Just ask him as he makes the rounds of this minute Art Deco lounge. If the dining room is full, try La

Rotonde across the foyer. After dinner, you can enjoy cocktails and live jazz in the Bebop bar. ◈ *Štěpánská 40 • 222 820038 • Dis. access • KKKKK*

Pálffy Palác

Enjoy the romantic ambience of Palffy Palace. Nestled in one of Prague Castle's imposing walls, this fine dining establishment offers something special with palatial surroundings and an expansive and ever-changing menu of traditional Czech and European cuisine. The menu features rich treats such as roasted veal sweetbreads with parmesan risotto or grilled duck breast with China sauce. A memorial dining experience with impeccable service *(see p89)*.

U Zlaté Studně

Plzeňská restaurace v Obecním domu

It may be a bit touristy, but nevertheless, gorgeous tiled mosaics of bucolic Bohemians cover the walls while an accordionist rolls out the Beer-Barrel Polka almost non-stop. The traditional food and beer are quite good and fairly priced. ◈ *Náměstí Republiky 5 • Map P3 • 222 002770 • Dis. access • KK*

Allegro

The Four Seasons' restaurant is the toast of the town even with other top restaurateurs. Expect highly attentive service and fine, authentic Italian cuisine by Milanese chef Vito Mollica. ◈ *Veleslavínova 2a • Map K3 • 221 427000 • Dis. access • KKKKK*

Country Life

Take heart, vegetarians, you haven't been forgotten. A meat-and dairy-free lunch buffet by day, *à la carte* menu for dinner, and it's all non-smoking. Pick up organic necessities at the adjoining shop. ◈ *Melantrichova 15 • Map L4 • 224 213366 • Dis. access • K*

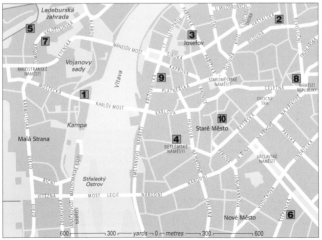

Left **Divadlo Alfred ve Dvoře** Right **Puppets, National Marionette Theatre**

TOP 10 Performing Arts Venues

Divadlo Archa

Divadlo Archa
Archa is Prague's premiere venue for avant-garde music, dance and movement theatre, recently hosting David Byrne and France's Compagnie Pál Frenák. ⊗ *Na Poříčí 26* • *Map P3*

Palác Akropolis
Žižkov's artsy appeal owes much to the Akropolis. International rock, jazz and world beat acts regularly appear on Akropolis's larger stages, while local bands crowd their guitars, trombones and violins on the smaller one *(see p66)*. ⊗ *Kubelíkova 33, Žižkov* • *Map B6*

Divadlo Alfred ve Dvoře
A community group recently came to the financial rescue to ensure this theatre continues hosting its outstanding non-verbal theatre. ⊗ *Františka Křížka 36, Holešovice* • *Map B5*

Ponec
Prague's new dance theatre has all aspects covered, from top international dance acts to workshops for young talent. ⊗ *Husitská 24a, Žižkov* • *Map B6*

Divadlo Na Zábradlí
Under Communism, it was playhouses such as this that gave vent to dissident thought. By staging daring works, they helped draw world attention to events such as the outspoken young playwright Václav Havel continually getting in trouble with the law. ⊗ *Anenské náměstí 5* • *Map M3*

Laterna Magika
This company was the main proponent behind Black-Light theatre, a genre in which black-clad actors, working against a black background, manipulate objects. See for yourself what all the fuss is about at their stage next to the National Theatre. ⊗ *Národní 4* • *Map E4*

Národní divadlo
The National Theatre's curtain first raised for Bedřich Smetana's opera *Libuše* in 1883; you can still see this or other Czech operas on the same stage today. Go to a performance, if only to appreciate the artistic work that went into creating the theatre. ⊗ *Národní 2* • *Map E4*

Ceiling, Národní divadlo

Auditorium, Rudolfinum

Rudolfinum

8 The Rudolfinum is home to the Czech Philharmonic. During World War II, the Nazis sought to remove Felix Mendelssohn from the gallery of statues on the roof. They inadvertently plucked Richard Wagner instead *(see p36)*. 🎵 *Náměstí Jana Palacha • Map K2*

Stavovské divadlo

9 The Estates Theatre is well-known as the venue where Mozart's *Don Giovanni* saw its first performance. It was also the first Czech-language playhouse in what was then a largely German-speaking city. The productions occasionally leave something to be desired, but if you don't see the *Don* here, then where? 🎵 *Ovocný trh 6 • Map M4*

Národní divadlo marionet

10 The National Marionette Theatre represents the pinnacle of the much-loved puppet genre, staging wonderful productions of Czech fairytales and other child-pleasing shows (in Czech). They also have the best Beatles tribute in town and a delightful marionette version of *Don Giovanni (see p54)*. 🎵 *Žatecká 1 • Map L3*

Top 10 Churches for Music Recitals

1 St Vitus's Cathedral
Prague Castle's cathedral is a spectacular setting for classical concerts *(see pp12–13)*.

2 St Agnes's Convent
This medieval convent regularly holds recitals *(see pp28–9)*.

3 Church of St Nicholas
Hosts chamber music recitals twice daily *(see p15)*.

4 St Nicholas's Church
Appreciate the Malá Strana church's Baroque grandeur at a concert of sacred music *(see p82)*.

5 Church of St James
This active house of worship regularly invites the general public to hear its organ *(see p74)*.

6 Mirror Chapel
The Baroque chamber of the Clementium hosts string quartets and other small ensembles *(see p74)*.

7 St Martin in the Wall
Organ and other recitals are on the bill at this Gothic church, once part of the Old Town defences. 🎵 *Martinská • Map L6*

8 Spanish Synagogue
The ornate 1880 organ figures in the sacred music concerts held in this opulent synagogue *(see p101)*.

9 St George's Basilica
Choral and string recitals present the greatest works of Mozart, Beethoven and other composers *(see p9)*.

10 Church of Sts Simon and Jude
Catch an ensemble of Prague Symphony Orchestra players in this Renaissance sanctuary. 🎵 *U milosrdných • Map F2*

Left **Radost** Right **Roxy**

TOP 10 Clubs

1 Radost
Prague's most chic disco pushes the limits with parties so hedonistic you wonder if there isn't a law against them. Hip-hop, funk and disco are the prevalent flavours on the dance floor. The vegetarian café upstairs is open until 4am. During peak lunch and dinner hours, it can be very hard to find a seat *(see p111)*.

2 Roxy
This former cinema is a must for fans of jungle and dub. Parties continue well into the morning, much to the dismay of the neighbours. Such live acts as the Asian Dub Foundation take the stage when it's not occupied by DJs or an experimental theatre production. A portion of Roxy's proceeds goes towards funding the Linhart Foundation, a non-profit organization whose aim is to promote contemporary art. Keep abreast of Roxy's events at http://klub.roxy.cz ◈ *Dlouhá 33 • Map M2*

3 Palác Akropolis
In addition to being at the heart of Prague's indie and world-music scene, the Palác Akropolis hosts the likes of Ani Difranco, Apollo 440 and Transglobal Underground. The small, smoky Divadelní bar is the hippest, hosting Prague's best DJs. On the ground floor level is a café and Czech restaurant. On a more cultural note, this is also the best venue in town to hear contemporary Romany music from such local acts as Alom or Věra Bílá and Kale. ◈ *Kubelíkova 33, Žižkov • Map B6*

4 Karlovy lázně
The former public bath-house, just 100 m from Charles Bridge, was converted into a dance club in the late 1990s. You can still admire the original tiles along the corridors and the splendid mosaic murals. Drained of water, the pools now serve as the dance floors. ◈ *Novotného lávka, Smetanovo nábřeží 198 • Map J5*

5 XT3
Žižkov's newest club resounds with dub and reggae most nights, while tough kids in jeans and hooded sweatshirts shuffle to the music or huddle over joints of marijuana. This is the best venue if you want to hear home-

Palác Akropolis

Radost's website at www.radostfx.cz outlines upcoming events at the club.

Karlovy lázně

grown hip-hop. It's also impossibly smoky, so don't wear anything that can't be washed or thrown away. 🅢 *Rokycanova 29, Žižkov • Map B6*

Mecca

The proprietors of Mecca have turned this former factory in the Holešovice warehouse district into a giant dance-and-dining emporium. The food is nouvelle cuisine, the crowd trendy and the parties wonderful. A little off the beaten track – take a taxi – but the trip is worth it. The restaurant serves food until 2am. 🅢 *U Průhonu 3, Holešovice • Map B5 • www.mecca.cz*

Jo's Garáž

A club chronicler in the mid-1990s wrote that Jo's had its finger on the pulse of Prague's "expat scene". Little has changed here since. The backpack set still bump eagerly to pop tunes on the cramped cellar dance floor. If you're hungry, upstairs is a restaurant serving passable Tex-Mex food. 🅢 *Malostranské náměstí 7 • Map C2*

U Malého Glena

The shoebox-sized cellar at "Little Glenn's" has to be Prague's smallest jazz venue. The music ranges from African-inspired drumming to blues to modern jazz, and most of it is of a high standard. Upstairs is a café where you can get

reasonable food and brunch at weekends. From the same entrepreneurs who brought you Bohemia Bagels *(see p88)*. 🅢 *Karmelitská 23 • Map C3*

Rock Café

Prague's music scene is teeming with so-called "revival bands", most of whom take the stage here and entertain audiences with tributes to everyone from Jimi Hendrix to Sade. There are also several bars, an internet café and a screening room where you can watch films of various past rock concerts. 🅢 *Národní 20 • Map L6*

Lucerna

Local "big-beat" acts are the mainstay at this Wenceslas Square music bar, but it occasionally hosts big names in jazz such as Maceo Parker, as well as where-are-they-now relics. (A separate adjoining venue, the Velkýw sál, or large hall, hosts bigger acts such as Wynton Marsalis.) The club's 1980s night is one of the biggest dance parties in town. 🅢 *Vodičkova 36 • Map F4*

Wall mural, XT3

Left **Karlovy Vary International Film Festival** Right **Prague Spring International Music Festival**

TOP 10 Festivals

1 Prague Spring International Music Festival

Bedřich Smetana's *Má vlast (My Country)* kicks off the annual three-week festival that draws classical music performers and fans from around the globe. The round of concerts closes with Beethoven's Ninth symphony.
🕓 *May–Jun*

2 Prague Autumn International Music Festival

Prague Spring's little sister has been running since 1991. Held in both Prague and Karlovy Vary, each year's festival begins with a vocal symphonic work, such as Beethoven's *Missa Solemnis* or Dvořák's *Requiem*. 🕓 *Sep*

3 Karlovy Vary International Film Festival

It's easier to hobnob with the stars here than at Cannes or Berlin. Hundreds of partygoers fairly turn the sleepy west Bohemian spa town upside down for 10 days. Hundreds of screenings, too. 🕓 *Jul*

4 May Day

The dawn finds young lovers dragging themselves home after a night of doing what comes naturally on Petřín Hill *(see pp32–3)*. While they sleep, their parents spend the national holiday trying to forget the old obligatory Communist rallies.
🕓 *1 May*

Street Theatre Festival

5 Street Theatre Festival

The creative minds behind the Alfred ve Dvoře theatre bring their trademark genre-bending artistry out of the theatre and parade it through the city centre on stilts. Offerings are both comic and macabre – much like the city itself. 🕓 *Sep*

6 Tanec Praha

This international dance festival is on the verge of becoming something great. The local dance scene has greatly benefited from it, and audiences can now see contemporary productions year-round. 🕓 *Jun*

7 Pardubice Steeplechase

With 39 jumps stretching over 7 km (4 miles), this is one of the biggest steeplechases in Europe. The first steeplechase here was held in 1874. 🕓 *Oct*

8 Prague Writer's Festival

Salman Rushdie, Susan Sontag and Elie Wiesel are just some of the internationally acclaimed authors who have attended this annual event. The organizers often get grief for giving Czech writers short shrift. ◈ *Apr*

9 Masopust

Czech swine start getting nervous in early February as the nation whets its appetite and knives for their version of Carnival. While the beer-and-pork orgies are more common in villages than in the big city, working-class Žižkov *(see p116)* throws a large party each year. ◈ *Shrove Tue*

10 Mikuláš, Vánoce, Silvestr

Czech Christmas celebrations are largely devoid of religion, but mulled wine starts flowing on St Nicholas's Day and doesn't stop until the Christmas carp is all eaten and New Year *(Silvestr)* fireworks arsenals are depleted. ◈ *Dec*

Christmas, Old Town Square

Top 10 National Holidays

1 New Year's Day
The day after *Silvestr* is quiet, after the New Year's celebrations. ◈ *1 Jan*

2 Easter Monday
Men give their women a gentle whipping with a willow switch. Ladies respond with eggs. ◈ *Mar–Apr*

3 Labour Day
Romantics lay flowers before the statue of Karel Hynech Macha on Petřín Hill. ◈ *1 May*

4 Day of Liberation
Plaques around town are adorned with flowers to remember those killed by the Germans in 1945. ◈ *8 May*

5 Cyril and Methodius Day
The Greek missionaries brought both Christianity and the Cyrillic alphabet to the Slavs *(see p39)*. ◈ *5 Jul*

6 Jan Hus Day
Czechs head for the hills where they roast sausages *(see p35)*. ◈ *6 Jul*

7 Czech Statehood Day
On St Wenceslas Day, as most Czechs call it, Bohemia's history is recalled. ◈ *28 Sep*

8 Independence Day
On this date in 1918 Czechoslovakia declared itself independent of Austro-Hungary. ◈ *28 Oct*

9 Day of the Fight for Freedom and Democracy
The anniversary of the 1989 Velvet Revolution. Candles and flowers are placed in various locations. ◈ *17 Nov*

10 Christmas
Streets fill with carp sellers and hedonists drinking mulled wine. ◈ *24–26 Dec*

AROUND TOWN

PRAGUE'S TOP 10

Left **House sign, Celetná** Centre **U Rotta, Old Town Square** Right **Clock, Old Town Hall**

Old Town

PRAGUE'S HEART IS A LAYERED CAKE OF HISTORY: *its oldest buildings have double cellars, owing to a flood-prevention programme that buried the original streets 3 m (10 ft) beneath those existing today; architecturally, it embraces every epoch from Romanesque to the Brutalist style of the Kotva department store. Historically, the burghers of the Old Town (Staré Město) were ill at ease with the castle, and vice versa, the town being a bastion of Protestant feistiness, and Old Town is still livelier than Hradčany – its cafés, clubs, restaurants and theatres keep the district buzzing around the clock.*

🔟 Sights

1. Old Town Square
2. Municipal House
3. Powder Gate
4. Celetná
5. Church of St James
6. Ungelt
7. Clementinum
8. Karlova
9. House of the Lords of Kunštát and Poděbrady
10. Bethlehem Square

Mosaic, Municipal House

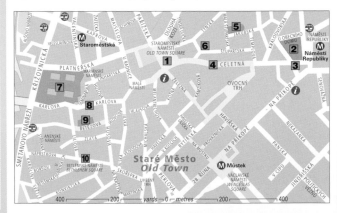

1 Old Town Square

Over the centuries, this now placid square at the heart of the city has witnessed hundreds of executions, political capitulations and, more recently of course, riotous ice hockey celebrations, a sport about which Czechs are fanatical. Today, the action is more likely to come from the crowds of tourists and Praguers, enjoying a coffee or a beer at one of the numerous pavement cafés. Dominated by the splendid Church of Our Lady before Týn, the square is always buzzing; in winter and summer, it's a wonderful place to watch the world go by (see pp14–17).

Church of Our Lady before Týn, Old Town Square

2 Municipal House

National Revival artist Alfons Mucha was one of many to lend his talents to the Municipal House (Obecní Dům), Prague's

Powder Gate

star Art Nouveau attraction. One of its most beautiful and striking features is Karel Špillar's mosaic above the main entrance, entitled Homage to Prague. It also has a firm place in history as it was from the Municipal House that Czechoslovakia was declared an independent state in 1918. Today, it is home to restaurants, cafés, exhibition halls, shops and the Prague Symphony Orchestra. ⊗ Náměstí Republiky 5 • Map P3 • 222 002121 • Open 10am–6pm daily • Adm

3 Powder Gate

In the 15th century, King Vladislav II laid the corner-stone for this tower at the city's eastern gate, intended to complement the Royal Court nearby. Used to store gunpowder in the 17th century, hence the name, the tower was damaged during attacks by Prussian forces in 1757. The Neo-Gothic façade seen today, with its sculptural decoration, dates from 1876. ⊗ Náměstí Republiky • Map P4 • Open Apr–Oct: 10am–6pm daily • Adm

Plaque, Clementium

Celetná
The medieval route from the silver-mining town of Kutná Hora in Bohemia passed down the street known today as Celetná, through Old Town Square and on to Prague Castle. There's still a lot of traffic on the gently curving street. ◈ Map N4

Church of St James
The Gothic and Baroque interior here wins the award for Prague's creepiest sanctuary. The church is best known for the

legend of the mummified arm hanging above the door (see p52), but visitors should not miss the opportunity to take in one of the organ recitals held here (see p65). ◈ Malá Štupartská • Map N3 • Open 9:30am–noon, 2–3:45pm Mon–Sat (except during Mass) • Free • Dis. access

Ungelt
Also known as Týn Courtyard, this was a fortified merchants settlement in the 11th century. The Baroque and Renaissance houses were completely renovated in the early 1990s, creating what is now one of the Old Town's most charming mercantile centres. ◈ Map M3

Clementinum
Built as a Jesuit college in the mid-17th century, the Clementinum now houses the National and State Technical libraries. The astronomer Johannes Kepler (see p35) discovered the laws of planetary motion atop the observatory tower. ◈ Křížovnické náměstí 4, Mariánské náměstí 5 & Seminářská 1 • Map K4 • 221 663111 • Library: Open 9am–7pm Mon–Fri, 8am–7pm Sat • Dis. access

Pietà carving, Church of St James

Karlova
8 You will inevitably get lost trying to follow "Charles Street" from Old Town Square to Charles Bridge; relax and enjoy the bewildering, twisting alleys choked with shops and cafés.
⊗ Map K4

House of the Lords of Kunštát and Poděbrady
9 George of Poděbrady lived here before he was elected king in 1458. The Romanesque "cellars" were ground-floor rooms until a flood-prevention programme raised the city's streets 3 m (10 ft). ⊗ Řetězová 3 • Map K5 • Open Apr–Oct: 11am–9pm daily • Adm

Bethlehem Square
10 The 15th-century Catholic reformer Jan Hus (see p35) preached in the reconstructed chapel on the square's north side. The original church was converted into apartments in the 18th century but had a loving restoration to its former state in the 1950s. ⊗ Map K5 • Chapel: Open Apr–Oct: 10am–6:30pm Tue–Sun; Nov–Mar: 10am–5:30pm Tue–Sun • Adm

Bethlehem Chapel, Bethlehem Square

A Stroll Around the Old Town

Morning

After breakfast at the **Municipal House** (see p73) café, take a guided tour of the building, then go and climb the **Powder Gate** (see p73) for the views next door before the caffeine wears off.

Wander down **Celetná**, ducking through the arcade to Štupartská and the **Church of St James**. If you have at least 45 minutes before the top of the hour, tour the **Old Town Hall** and watch the Apostles' show on the Astronomical Clock from backstage (see pp16–17). Otherwise, shop in the **Ungelt** and join the crowd below the clock outside, to see the spectacle.

For lunch, head to the **Century** restaurant (see p79) for some delicious modern European food.

Afternoon

Circumnavigate **Old Town Square** (see pp14–15) before entering the meandering turns of **Karlova** and wandering leisurely past the area's old buildings to **Bethlehem Square**. Have a tour of the lovely Bethlehem Chapel, then find your way back to Karlova to visit the **Clementinum**.

Alternately, if you're now a little on the tired side, have a coffee at **Café de Paris** (see p78) before freshening up for dinner. If you're heading to the theatre or a concert, curtains go up around 7:30pm, so it is sensible to dine afterwards.

Left **Blue** Right **Dr Stuart's Botanicus**

TOP 10 Shops

Blue
A dazzlingly different kind of glass shop. Modern, fun designs in bowls and other knick-knacks, as well as T-shirts and other tourist fare *(see p57)*. ⬧ *Malé náměstí 14 • Map L4*

Moser
Classic crystal and cut glass produced by this well-known manufacturer. Even if you're not interested in a large vase or a crystal hedgehog, it's worth a look around. ⬧ *Malé náměstí 11 • Map L4*

Charles University Gift Shop
Looking for cool souvenirs to take back for the kids? Problem solved: a Charles University pullover. If it's chilly out, you'll want one for yourself as well. ⬧ *Celetná 24 • Map M3*

Franz Kafka Bookshop
Here you can find a wide range of Czech literature in translation, coffee-table books and catalogues from recent exhibitions next door at the Municipal Gallery, plus classical music CDs. ⬧ *Staroměstské náměstí 12 • Map M3*

U rytíře Kryštofa
Perhaps only in Prague would you find a weird treasure trove such as this. Battle-axes, broadswords and maces, not to mention chastity belts and breastplates. ⬧ *Kožná 8 • Map M4*

Dr Stuart's Botanicus
The store's all-natural health and beauty products are produced at a "historic village" east of Prague; enquire about tours. Herbs, oils and other seasonings, too *(see p56)*. ⬧ *Týn 3 • Map M3*

Antikvariát U Karlova mostu
This shop originally served as a customs house from as early as the 10th century. An antiquarian bookshop, it continues to buy and offers old and rare prints, Czech and foreign literature, Renaissance and Baroque maps and decorative graphics. ⬧ *Týn 2 • Map M3*

Czech Folk Crafts (Manufaktura)
Kids these days might not appreciate the handmade wooden toys or corn-husk dolls, but when was the last time you bought yourself a gift? ⬧ *Karlova 26 • Map L4*

Art Decoratif
An Art Nouveau shop with a fine selection of Alfons Mucha reproductions, jewellery and lamps from the era. ⬧ *Melantrichova 5 • Map M5*

Keramika
Probably every Czech kitchen has at least one of these ceramic plates. The traditional folk patterns are either blue, red or yellow. ⬧ *Havelská 21 • Map M5*

Left **Karlovy lázně** Right **Jazz Club Zelezná**

TOP10 Nightclubs

1 Misch-Masch
Party with the locals with all-night dancing and drinking at this revived club. The four dance floors, along with big name international DJs make this a popular venue. ◈ *Veletržní 61*

2 Karlovy lázně
Bruce Willis jammed here when in town. Weekends find a queue of young clubbers stretching along the river bank waiting to get in to these remodelled municipal baths. Four levels of clubbing, from classic rock to DJs and, occasionally, live bands. ◈ *Novotného lávka • Map J5*

3 Roxy
The Old Town's most exciting club. In addition to the best dance parties in town, the former cinema hosts experimental theatre, live bands and art exhibitions. ◈ *Dlouhá 33 • Map M3*

4 M1
This "secret lounge" in the Old Town is perfectly suited to trendy kids in the know. It is open nightly, and the varied musical offers reflect the social mix. ◈ *Masná 1 • Map M3*

5 Vagon
One of the originals for exciting live music, this place hosts blues or rock bands most nights, with a mix of well-known and unsigned acts. Always a lively atmosphere ◈ *Národní 25 • Map L6*

6 Radost FX
A hit with locals, as well as college kids and tourists, Radox serves up an eclectic mix of DJ nights, theme parties, fashion shows and go-go dancers. ◈ *Bělehradská 120 • Map G6*

7 Cross Club
This quirky club with moving metal sculptures has remnants of its grungy beginnings. It plays host to varied DJs and bands. ◈ *Plynární 23*

8 Friends
The name fits. Prague's best gay cocktail bar has a steady following among expat and local men who are less interested in cruising than in just having a drink with like-minded folks. The owner Michael will tell you what's what. ◈ *Bartolomějská 11 • Map K6*

9 Jazz Club Železná (Mecca)
Some of the city's edgiest jazz artists take to the stage at this club. Železná has left its entertaining labyrinthine venue and moved to Mecca, in Holešovice *(see p67)*. Table service remains a bit off-hand. ◈ *U Průhonu 3 • Map B5*

10 Jazz Club U Staré paní
Prague's favourite jazz club may not look like much from the outside, but the best local acts perform here regularly to full houses. Relatively high cover charges can't keep fans away. ◈ *Michalská 9 • Map L5*

Left **Café Obecní dům** Right **Café de Paris**

TOP10 Cafés and Pubs

1 Café Obecní dům
Dressed to the nines in Art Nouveau splendour, the Municipal House café glitters. Stop in for breakfast. ⊗ *Náměstí Republiky 5 • Map P3*

2 Café de Paris
If you're not already staying at the Hotel Paříž, you may be tempted to take a room just so you can have your morning coffee in this Jugendstil café. Superior service. ⊗ *Hotel Paříž, U Obecního domu 1 • Map P3*

3 Le Patio
A new sushi bar heightens the trendy feeling at this "world-beat" café. There is an extensive dinner menu with classic French dishes as well as Czech specialities. Open for breakfast and lunch, with live bands in the evenings. ⊗ *Národní 22 • Map L6 • 224 934402 • Dis. access • KKK*

4 Ebel Coffeehouse
You won't find a better cup of coffee in the city than at Ebel, using beans from all over the world. A stone's throw from Old Town Square in the Ungelt courtyard. ⊗ *Týn 2 • Map M3*

5 Týnská Literární kavárna
The local customers here are serious about their literature, at this café attached to a bookstore. The hidden courtyard is a blissfully quiet space to enjoy a beer on summer nights. ⊗ *Týnská 6 • Map M3*

6 Grand Café Praha
Unlike other establishments on the square, this coffee house actually offers great value and good service. ⊗ *Staroměstské náměstí 22 • Map M3*

7 Hotel U Prince
Have an unforgettable dining experience on the roof top terrace of Hotel U Prince. Serves as both a restaurant and café . ⊗ *Staroměstské náměstí 29 • Map L4 • 224 213807*

8 Café Indigo
Cafe Indigo caters for all tastes with a range of sweet and savoury pancakes, pasta dishes and vegetarian options. Breakfast is also served. ⊗ *Platnéřská 11 • Map K4 • 731 216035 • Dis. access*

9 Hotel Evropa
Have traditional coffee and cakes in the heart of the city centre. ⊗ *Václavské náměstí 25 • Map N6 • 224 215387 • Dis. access*

10 Atmoška (Atmosphere)
This café, pub and restaurant has ultimate views of the castle and Charles Bridge. ⊗ *Smetanovo nábřeží 14 • Map J5*

Recommend your favourite café on traveldk.com

Price Categories

For a three-course meal for one with half a bottle of wine (or equivalent meal), taxes and extra charges.

K	under Kč300
KK	Kč300–Kč500
KKK	Kč500–Kč700
KKKK	Kč700–Kč1000
KKKKK	over Kč1000

Above **La Provence**

🔟 Places to Eat

1 Sarah Bernhardt
French cuisine in an opulent Art Nouveau setting inspired by Alfons Mucha's paintings of the French actress. Bohumil Hrabal *(see p45)* celebrated the hotel in his novel *I Served the King of England*. ⊗ *Hotel Paříž, U Obecního domu 1 • Map P3 • 222 195900 •* **KKK**

2 Century
Order a Marlene Dietrich (stuffed avacado with Roquefort and marzipan) or an Al Capone (roast chicken with hot salsa) in this intimate restaurant. ⊗ *Karoliny Světle 34 • Map E4 •* **KKK**

3 La Provence
Very good southern French cuisine – try the rabbit – in a boisterous setting. The Banana Café upstairs offers go-go dancers and occasional drag shows. ⊗ *Štupartská 9 • Map M3 • 222 324801 •* **KKK**

4 Kogo
Serving superior Italian dishes at remarkably low prices, Kogo is wildly popular with discerning locals; book ahead. The service is marvellous. ⊗ *Havelská 27 • Map M5 • 224 214543 •* **KK**

5 Divinis
This high-end wine bar and restaurant manages to balance a modern feel with a traditional Italian atmosphere. Good quality wines compliment the classic Sicilian specialties. ⊗ *Týnská 19 • Map M3 • 224 808318 •* **KK**

6 Bellevue
A gorgeous view of the castle rising above Charles Bridge, and formal, Continental dining. ⊗ *Smetanovo nábřeží 18 • Map J5 • 222 221443 •* **KKKK**

7 Klub architektů
Situated in a medieval cellar, this casual club specializes in *"eintopf"* dishes such as beef strips with sour cream and apples. ⊗ *Betlémské náměstí 5a • Map K5 • 224 401214 •* **KK**

8 Lehka Hlava
This vegetarian restaurant has a varied menu. It's so good you don't even notice there are no meat choices. ⊗ *Boršov 2 • Map K5 • 222 220665 •* **KK**

9 DaNico
This wine bar combines good quality Italian food with outstanding wines. ⊗ *Dlouhá 21 • Map M3 • 222 311807 •* **KKK**

10 Modrý Zub
Fast Thai food at its best, for a quick snack or light meal. Huge windows make for great people watching. ⊗ *Jindřišská 5 • Map P6 • 222 212622 • Dis. access •* **K**

Note: *Unless otherwise stated, all restaurants accept credit cards and serve vegetarian meals*

Left **House of the Two Suns, Nerudova** Right **View from Petřín Hill**

Malá Strana

MALÁ STRANA, NOW KNOWN AS THE "LITTLE QUARTER", *was originally called the New Town, a century before Charles IV moved that name across the river (see pp104–13). Floods, fires and war kept construction busy on the Vltava's left bank; few of the original Romanesque and Gothic buildings remain. During the Habsburgs' reign, grand palaces were built in Baroque style, but these went to ruin when the nobility left; modern developers are attempting to restore them. Today, the area is an enclave of parks, cafés, winding streets and unassuming churches.*

🔟 Sights

1. Charles Bridge
2. Petřín Hill
3. Nerudova
4. John Lennon Wall
5. Malostranské náměstí
6. St Nicholas's Church
7. Kampa Island
8. Maltézské náměstí
9. Church of Our Lady Victorious
10. Vojanovy sady

Čertovka, Kampa Island

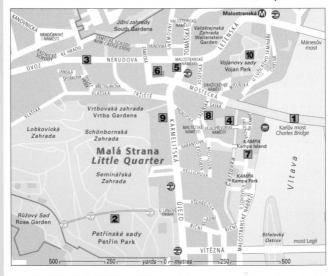

Charles Bridge at sunset

Charles Bridge

For almost all visitors to Prague, this spectacular Gothic bridge, crossing the Vltava from the Old Town to the castle complex, remains their most memorable image of the city, long after they have returned home *(see pp18–19)*.

Petřín Hill

A more than welcome respite from the tiny, generally crowded streets in the city below is Prague's sprawling park, looking down over spires and rooftops. Enjoy the views all the way up the hill by taking the funicular train *(see pp32–3)*.

Original John Lennon Wall

Nerudova

The 19th-century Czech writer and poet Jan Neruda (1834–91) lived in the "House of the Two Suns", at the top of the street that now bears his name. Lined with former palaces, Nerudova leads uphill from Malostranské náměstí, its many winding side streets leading visitors up to Prague Castle *(see pp8–11)*. Traditionally an artists' quarter, the street is worth exploring for its many craft shops and galleries. It is also home to one of the most concentrated collections of historichouse signs in the city *(see pp42–3)*. ◈ Map C2

John Lennon Wall

Prague hippies and the secret police once waged a long-running paint battle here, as the latter constantly tried to eradicate the graffiti artists' work. The original artwork, created by a Mexican student after Lennon's assassination, has been painted over many times *(see p53)*, but the so-called John Lennon Peace Club still gathers annually at this self-made shrine to sing the former Beatle's songs and praises. ◈ Velkopřevorské náměstí • Map D3

St Nicholas's Church

Malostranské náměstí

The hectic traffic that now detracts from the beauty of Malá Strana's main square seems historically fitting – in the past it has been witness to innumerable destructive fires, revolutions, including the 1618 defenestration *(see p11)*, and executions during the days when a gallows stood here. St Nicholas's Church and the adjoining Jesuit college dominate the centre of the square, while lovely Neo-Classical palace arcades and restaurants line the perimeter. One of the most important buildings is the Směmovna palace, once the headquarters of the National Assembly, and now home to the Chamber of Deputies. ◈ *Map C2*

St Nicholas's Church

Jesuits constructed this stunning example of Baroque architecture in the early 18th century. It was designed by the acclaimed Baroque architects, Christoph and Kilian Dientzenhofer, while other prominent artists adorned the interior with exquisite carvings, statues and frescoes. Visitors can see examples of the interior's painstaking reconstruction which took place in the 1950s, and enjoy the view from the clock tower *(see p39)*. ◈ *Malostranské náměstí • Map C2 • Open Apr–Oct 9am–5pm, Nov–Mar 9am–4pm daily • Adm*

Kampa Island

The tiny Čertovka (Devil's Canal) that separates Kampa from Malá Strana was once the town's "laundry", milling area and, in the 17th century, home to a thriving pottery industry. A popular park now covers the island's southern end *(see p40)* while the

Malostranské náměstí

Kampa Island

northern half is home to elegant embassies, restaurants and hotels. Much of the island was submerged during the 2002 flooding and many buildings had to be repaired. 🕲 *Map D3*

8 Maltézské náměstí

The Knights of Malta once had an autonomous settlement here, and the square still bears their name. The area is dominated by beautiful Baroque palaces, and the 12th-century Church of Our Lady Below the Chain – so called for the Marian portrait inside that hangs beneath chains from the Judith Bridge, the precursor to Charles Bridge. 🕲 *Map C3*

9 Church of Our Lady Victorious

More popularly known as the Church of the Infant Jesus of Prague, Prague's first Baroque church (1611) got its name – and its Catholic outlook – after the Battle of White Mountain *(see p34)*. Visitors stream in to the church to see the miracle-working statue of the Christ Child *(see p38)*. 🕲 *Karmelitská 9 • Map C3*

10 Vojanovy sady

Malá Strana has many green pockets, but Vojan's gardens top them all for their romantic charm. Tulip beds, flowering fruit trees and the occasional peacock add to the fairytale atmosphere *(see p40)*. 🕲 *U lužického semináře • Map D2*

A Day in Malá Strana

Morning

🕐 You can approach the Little Quarter from the Old Town as royal processions once did, by crossing **Charles Bridge** *(see pp18–19)*, or you can save your energy for the day ahead, and start from the top of the hill and walk down. Get to **Nerudova** *(see p81)* from one of the many side streets leading from Hradčany and stroll down, window shopping at the many craft outlets on your way. Don't worry if you stray off the beaten path; as long as you continue downhill, you'll end up at the area's central hub, **Malostranské náměstí**. Here, spend at least an hour savouring one of the city's most spectacular buildings, **St Nicholas's Church**.

Pause for lunch, either at one of the many cheap cafés on Malostranské náměstí or splash out at **Kampa Park** *(see p89)*.

Afternoon

After lunch, take Tomášská and Valdštejnská around to the **Wallenstein Garden** *(see p40)*. Tip-toe through the tulips at **Vojanovy sady** and continue down U lužického semináře under Charles Bridge and onto **Kampa Island**.

After coffee at **Café Čertovka***(see p88)*, check the writing on the **John Lennon Wall** *(see p81)* before wrapping up at the **Church of Our Lady Victorious**.

In the evening, catch a recital at St Nicholas's Church or dance the night away with the young crowd at **Jo's Garáž** *(see p67)*.

Following pages: **Kampa Island**

Left **Thun-Hohenstein Palace** Centre **Wallenstein Palace** Right **Shoenborn Palace**

Palaces

Nostitz Palace
Have a look at the recent restoration work at this 17th-century palace while taking in a chamber music concert. The Nostitz family lent their name to the playhouse now known as the Estates Theatre. ◈ *Maltézské náměstí 1 • Map C3*

Thun-Hohenstein Palace
The Kolowrat family's heraldic eagles support the portal of this palace. Built by Giovanni Santini-Aichel in 1726, the building is now the Italian Embassy. ◈ *Nerudova 20 • Map C2*

Lichtenstein Palace
Originally several houses, Lichtenstein Palace fused in the 16th century. Today, it is home to Prague's Academy of Music and numerous concerts and recitals. ◈ *Malostranské náměstí 13 • Map C2*

Morzin Palace
Two giant Moors (hence Morzin) bearing up the Romanian Embassy's façade are said to wander about Malá Strana streets at night. ◈ *Nerudova 5 • Map C2*

Wallenstein Palace
General Wallenstein pulled out all the stops creating what is essentially a monument to himself. On the palace's frescoes, the Thirty Years' War commander had himself depicted as both Achilles and Mars. ◈ *Valdštejnské náměstí 4 • Map D2*

Buquoy Palace
This pink stucco palace and the John Lennon Wall are separated by only a few steps, but they are miles apart aesthetically. However, the French Ambassador helped preserve the graffiti opposite his offices in the 1980s. ◈ *Velkopřevorské náměstí 2 • Map D3*

Michna Palace
Architect Francesco Caratti modelled this palace on Versailles. Today it's home to the Museum of Physical Culture and Sport. ◈ *Újezd 40 • Map C4*

Shoenborn Palace
Czechoslovakia's first ambassador to the United States sold the palace to the US government in 1925. Count Colloredo-Mansfeld owned the palace in the 17th century: having lost a leg in the Thirty Years' War, he had the stairs reconstructed so he could ride his horse into the building. ◈ *Tržiště 15 • Map C3*

Lobkowitz Palace
Home to the German Embassy; in 1989 hundreds of East Germans found their way to the West by scrambling over the embassy's back fence. ◈ *Vlašská 19 • Map C3*

Kaunitz Palace
The Yugoslav Embassy sat quietly in its pink and yellow stucco for more than 300 years until war made it a popular spot for protests. ◈ *Mostecká 15 • Map D3*

There is another Lichtenstein Palace on Kampa Island, but they are helpful to concertgoers who get the two confused.

Left **Clothes shop in Malá Strana** Right **Gallery Bambino di Praga**

🔟 Shops

1 Obchod pod lampou
One of the scores of marionettes on sale here would make a great souvenir, since Prague is an international centre for marionette theatre. The helpful staff can teach you basic techniques of string-pulling.
◎ *U lužického semináře 5 • Map D2*

2 Turkish Tea Room
They say Prague's first café was owned by a Turk; this isn't it. Drop in anyway for a cup of proper Turkish coffee or other delights, then buy some coffee to take home. ◎ *Úvoz 1 • Map B2*

3 U bílého jablka
If you can't bring yourself to leave Prague, take it with you: this shop sells adorable ceramic miniatures of the surrounding houses and other monuments.
◎ *Úvoz 1 • Map B2*

4 Galerie Boema
The gifts and reproductions here run from merely eccentric to downright creepy. Take home a Torah pointer or scale replicas of gargoyles from St Vitus's Cathedral. ◎ *Nerudova 49 • Map C2*

5 American Heating
Around the corner from the US Embassy is a shop specializing in restoration and sales of historical stoves. Great news if you want to export Malá Strana's coal-scented atmosphere home with you. ◎ *Karmelitská 21 • Map C3*

6 Mýrnyx Týrnyx
Hipsters can pick up Prague's best club and retro fashions here, as well as expert clubbing advice from the friendly owner Maya Květný. ◎ *Saská • Map D3*

7 Květinářstvi u Červeného lva
It appears as if a jungle is sprouting from the hole in the wall that is the "Flowershop at the Red Lion". Spruce up your apartment or hotel room with their unique arrangements. ◎ *Saská • Map D3*

8 National House of Wine
This serves as a public wine exposition representing the Czech wine industry to both Czech and foreign visitors. You can even take part in their educational activities and wine tasting programmes. ◎ *Mostecká 19 • Map C3*

9 Gallery Bambino di Praga
The souvenir shop across the street from the Church of Our Lady Victorious, named after the miracle child *(see p83)*, raised many eyebrows when they claimed to have coined the word "Pokémon"– an acronym, they say, for their slogan "Power of the Bambino Keep up the Monde". ◎ *Karmelitská 12 • Map C3*

10 Vetešnictví
A favourite junk shop, where you can find everything from silver teaspoons to glass and door handles. ◎ *Vítězná 16 • Map C4*

Left **Bohemia Bagel** Right **Hospůdka Na Čevtovce**

Cafés and Pubs

Bohemia Bagel
It's hard to believe now, but Prague had no bagels until American entrepreneurs opened this shop here in 1997, serving fresh-baked bagels, sandwiches and endless cups of coffee. Open late. ® *Lázeňská 19 • Map C3*

Hospůdka Na Čevtovce
This Kampa Island pub serves good beer and coffee at a fraction of the price found on the other side of the block. ® *Hroznová 6 • Map D3*

U zeleného čaje
Serving imported teas, sandwiches and salads, "At the Green Tea" offers a welcome change from the ubiquitous beer and fried food. ® *Nerudova 19 • Map C2*

Cafe Čertovka
The stairway leading to this café's riverside patio is so narrow it needs its own traffic lights. They say President Václav Havel took Pink Floyd here for beer. ® *U lužického semináře • Map D2*

Bar Bar
The salads, waffles and crêpes served here make an excellent light lunch, but you'll have trouble finding a seat in the evening. ® *Všehrdova 17 • Map C4*

U Kocoura
You might think the regulars at this pub on Malá Strana's main drag would be used to tourists by now, but don't be surprised if every face turns to meet you. Serves excellent Pilsner. ® *Nerudova 2 • Map C2*

Chiméra
With its threadbare furniture and oil lamps on every table, this café is made for rainy nights. In chilly weather, try their excellent mulled wine. ® *Lázeňská 6 • Map D3*

U Maltéze
The cold Budvar served here is the best. If they're serving homemade sausage, don't miss it. ® *Maltézské náměstí 3 • Map C3*

U Zlatého hada
This tiny wine cellar sells excellent imported and domestic wines. If the tables out front are full, take your bottle to Petřín Hill. ® *Maltézské náměstí 15 • Map C3*

St Nicholas Café
St Nick's is the expat bar of choice in Malá Strana. From the corner table in the back, you can hear absinthe-induced whispers bouncing off the vaulted ceiling. ® *Tržiště 10 • Map C3*

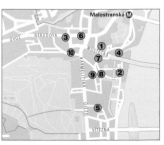

Around Town – Malá Strana

Price Categories
For a three-course meal for one with half a bottle of wine (or equivalent meal), taxes and extra charges.
K under Kč300
KK Kč300–Kč500
KKK Kč500–Kč700
KKKK Kč700–Kč1000
KKKKK over Kč1000

🔟 Restaurants

1 Cantina
The best Mexican food in Prague. The *fajitas* are great; try the chicken and banana variety. Book ahead. ⊗ *Újezd 38 • Map C4 • 257 317173 • Dis. access •* **KK**

2 Pálffy Palác
This fine-dining establishment with a view of the castle terraces seems to revel in its tattered splendour. ⊗ *Valdštejnská 14 • Map D2 • 257 530522 •* **KKKK**

3 C'est La Vie
Enjoy riverside dining in the warmer months at this fancy French eatery. The menu includes fresh fish and seafood as its speciality. ⊗ *Říční 1 • Map D4 • 257 321511 • Dis. access •* **KKKK**

4 U Patrona
The Continental and Czech cuisine will please gourmets; the balcony overlooking Charles Bridge will delight romantics. ⊗ *Dražického náměstí 4 • Map D3 • 257 530725 •* **KKKK**

5 U Maltézských rytířů
For a local treat, have the venison Chateaubriand. ⊗ *Prokopská 10 • Map C3 • 257 530075 • No vegetarian options •* **KKKK**

6 Kampa Park
This top-rated riverside restaurant serves a mix of Continental classics and fusion cuisine. ⊗ *Na Kampě 8b • Map D3 • 800 152672 • Dis. access •* **KKKKK**

7 Gitanes
This restaurant offers the best of Dalmatian, Greek, Southern European and North African cooking. ⊗ *Tržiště 7 • Map C3 • 257 530163 •* **KKK**

8 The Little Whale (U malé velryby)
The Little Whale offers new twists on old classics in an affordable "Czech brasserie" style. With plenty of choices from calamari to steaks and the special Little Whale seafood pie. ⊗ *Maltézské náměstí 15 • Map C3 • 257 214703 • Dis. access •* **KK**

9 Malostranská restaurace
Good pub food. If cigarette smoke bothers you, look elsewhere. ⊗ *Karmelitská 25 • Map C3 • 257 531418 • Dis. access •* **K**

10 El Centro
The Spanish owners and imported chefs make sure the *paella* is just right, at this authentic and popular eatery. ⊗ *Maltézské náměstí 9 • Map C3 • 257 533343 • Dis. access •* **K**

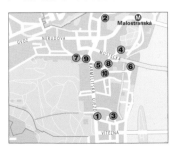

Note: Unless otherwise stated, all restaurants accept credit cards and serve vegetarian meals

89

Left **Loreto** Right **Belvedere, Royal Gardens**

Prague Castle and Hradčany

FOUNDED BY PRINCE BOŘIVOJ IN THE 9TH CENTURY, *Prague Castle and its attendant cathedral tower above the city from the long hill known as Hradčany. The surrounding town was founded in 1320, becoming home to servants' hovels and, after the cataclysmic fire of 1541, grand palaces. Baroque and Renaissance reconstructions in the area created much of what visitors see today. The Loreto shrine to the Virgin Mary demonstrated the growing importance of Prague to the Church. At the castle, primitive defences were removed, making room for gardens, parade grounds and other needs of a modern empire. When the Habsburgs removed the imperial seat to Vienna, Hradčany seemed to become preserved in time, saving it from the ravages of war and modernization. The area abounds with interesting sights for art and history lovers, as well as romantic hidden lanes and parks – in short, a total expression of the Czech nation's shifting epochs and politics.*

Golden Lane

🔟 Sights

1 Prague Castle	**6** Nový Svět
2 St Vitus's Cathedral	**7** Monument to Victims of Police Torture
3 Loreto	**8** Old Castle Steps
4 Royal Gardens	**9** Hradčanské náměstí
5 New Castle Steps	**10** Radnické schody

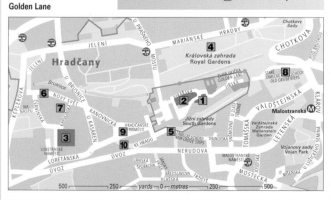

Sign up for DK's email newsletter on traveldk.com

Prague Castle in winter

1 Prague Castle

The first and main focus of most tourists' visit to Prague is the gloriously ornate and varied castle complex *(see pp8–11)*. Its determined survival in the face of an often turbulent history only seems to add to its attractiveness and fascination. Despite its medieval appearance, however, it is still as much of a political stronghold as it has always been, as the seat of the modern-day Czech government, overseen by President Václav Klaus whose office is here.

Golden Portal, St Vitus's Cathedral

2 St Vitus's Cathedral

The Gothic splendour of St Vitus's spires can be seen from almost every vantage point in Prague, but don't miss the opportunity to see its beautiful stained-glass windows and gargoyles close up *(see pp12–13)*.

3 Loreto

The onion-domed white towers of this 17th-century church complex are like something out a fairytale, but it's up to you whether you choose to believe in the reconstruction of the Virgin Mary's house, the Santa Casa, at the heart of the building *(see pp20–21)*.

4 Royal Gardens

Visitors may regret the disappearance of the maze and pineapple trees that once featured here, but will likely appreciate the absence of Rudolph II's lions. Within the English-style garden are the former Presidential Residence (the First Lady didn't like it), the sgraffitoed Ball Game Hall and the Royal Summer Palace, also known as Belvedere. ◎ *U Prašného mostu • Map C1 • Open May–Oct: 10am–6pm daily • Dis. access • Free*

5 New Castle Steps

The Royal Route, established in the 15th century for the coronation of George of Poděbrady, covered the distance from the Municipal House on the Old Town Square (see p73) to the castle. The last stretch climbed the hill right about here, although the original

Nový Svět

steps were reconstructed during Empress Maria Theresa's Hradčany renovation in the 18th century. Halfway up is a music pavilion, from which a brass quartet of the Castle Guard serenades the city each morning at 10am. ◉ Map C2

6 Nový Svět

Nestled below the Loreto (see pp20–21) and at the head of the Stag Moat is Nový Svět (New World), perhaps the best street in town for romantic strolling, weather permitting. The picturesque low houses were built in the 17th century to replace the medieval slums built for castle workers after the former burned down in 1541. They remain unchanged by time, still displaying their decorative house signs. Rudolph II's choleric astronomer Tycho de Brahe (see p35) lived at No. 1 and apparently found the noise of nearby churchbells insufferable. ◉ Map A2

7 Monument to Victims of Police Torture

It seems a cruel joke, but the Communist secret police had an interrogation centre in this picture-postcard neighbourhood. The plaque on the wall at Kapucínská 2 honours those who were brought here and coerced into compromising themselves, their neighbours and even their family. ◉ Map A2

8 Old Castle Steps

The relatively gentle slope of the Prague Castle's "back-door" entrance leads from the Malostranská metro to the castle's eastern gate. Local

Old Castle Steps

Stag Moat

When the Stag Moat was not fulfilling its defensive duties, Prague's rulers used it as a hunting park. Rudolph II is said to have been particularly fond of chasing deer around the narrow, wooded gorge with his pet lions. The Powder Bridge's earthworks were recently excavated to permit pedestrians access to both halves of the moat.

---

artists and artisans line the steps, selling everything from watercolour prints to polished stones. Below the steps are terraced gardens. ✪ *Map D2*

9 Hradčanské náměstí

Many visitors enter this square backwards, trying to fit St Vitus's spires in their viewfinders. Tear your eyes away from the castle's western face and you'll see, among other Renaissance buildings, the colourful Archbishop's Palace and the grim Schwarzenberg Palace across the way. In the green centre is a plague column from 1726; opposite the castle is the Toskánský Palace, now the Ministry of Foreign Affairs. ✪ *Map B2*

10 Radnické schody

The Courthouse Steps lead from Hradčany's former mayoral residence, now the hotel Zlatá Hvězda, to the old courthouse at Loretánská 1. At the bottom are two statues, St John of Nepomuk on the left and what appears to be St Joseph in Renaissance garb on the right. There are more steps than is immediately apparent, making the pub halfway up a convenient stop-off point. ✪ *Map B2*

Hradčanské náměstí

A Day in Hradčany

Morning

Start your day with a brisk climb up the **New Castle Steps**, and time your ascent to hear the 10am Castle Guard brass quartet. Leaving the castle behind you, walk west through **Hradčanské náměstí**. As you pass the Schwarzenberg Palace, check to see if the reinstallation of the Military History Museum is complete – if so, take a look at the exhibitions of weapons and uniforms (*Hradčanské náměstí 2 • Map B2 • 220 202020 • Open daily • Adm*).

Now walk up Loretánská to Loretánské náměstí, where you'll find the vast Černín Palace staring down at the lovely **Loreto** (*see pp20–21*). Explore the latter and its odd gallery of saints before lunch next door at **Restaurant U Lorety** (*see p97*).

Afternoon

Exit Loretánské náměstí past the Capuchin monastery and follow Černínská downhill, pausing on **Nový Svět**. Coo over the street's piebald houses and follow Kanovnická back to Hradčanské náměstí.

The rest of the afternoon will be taken up with a tour of the unmissable **Prague Castle** (*see pp8–11*), **St Vitus's Cathedral** (*see pp12–13*), and the myriad of other attractions in the castle complex.

To end the day, find your way back to Loretánské náměstí 1 and the famed pub **U Černého vola** (*see p96*) for a pickled sausage and a glass of beer.

Following pages: **View of Prague and the Vltava from Hradčany**

Left **U Černého vola** Right **Hospůdka na schodech**

🔟 Pubs and Cafés

1 U Černého vola
Part of the proceeds from the pub "At the Black Ox" go to help the nearby school for the blind. Watching the regulars knock back litre after litre of beer, you can see why. ◈ *Loretánské náměstí 1 • Map A2*

2 Hospůdka na schodech
The "Little Pub on the Steps" seems strategically located to relieve exhausted tourists climbing Radnické schody *(see p93)*. Inexpensive, and popular with the locals. ◈ *Radnické schody 5 • Map B2*

3 Café Poet
An out-of-the-way, peaceful café in the castle's Gardens on the Bastion, where you can rest over a cup of tea or coffee. Light snacks, too. ◈ *Zahrada na Baště, Prague Castle • Map C1*

4 Kajetánka
Sip an *espresso* on the rooftop while peering through one of the telescopes at the city below. The quiet patio has large tables where you can lunch and plan your visit to the castle next door. ◈ *Ke Hradu • Map C1*

5 U Labutí
"The Swan" serves Pilsner Urquell and some substantial dishes, such as *wiener schnitzel* and goulash, on its garden terrace overlooking the upper Stag Moat. ◈ *Hradčanské náměstí 11 • Map B2*

6 Café Savoy
This café feels just like a Prague café should, with high ceilings, elegant fixtures and huge windows. Along with a standard menu, the café also has a gourmet menu and offers a selection of pastries to enjoy with a coffee. ◈ *Vítězná 5 • Map C4*

7 Tosca
Under the southern arcade of the Toskánský Palace is a gracious pizzeria and Italian café where you can break the dumpling habit. The building is the Ministry of Foreign Affairs, after all. ◈ *Hradčanské náměstí 5 • Map B2*

8 Lobkovický Palace
This pleasant and smart restaurant offers light lunches and suppers with a view of the city. The café in the courtyard is the place to end your tour of the castle. ◈ *Jiřská 3 • Map C2*

9 Café Gallery
In the narrow alleys leading into Golden Lane are a number of pavement cafés offering coffees, sandwiches, wine and spirits. Outdoor seating in good weather. ◈ *Zlatá ulička u Daliborky 42 • Map C1*

10 Gallery Café
Visitors can escape the crowds at this café hidden in the arcade on the way to the castle. Relax with coffee and strudel, or beer and sandwiches. ◈ *Lovetánská 3 • Map B2*

Price Categories

For a three-course meal for one with half a bottle of wine (or equivalent meal), taxes and extra charges.	**K** under Kč300 **KK** Kč300–Kč500 **KKK** Kč500–Kč700 **KKKK** Kč700–Kč1000 **KKKKK** over Kč1000

Above **Hradčany Restaurant**

TOP 10 Restaurants

1 Hradčany Restaurant
This fine-dining restaurant at the Hotel Savoy serves a sushi buffet every Sunday from noon to 2pm. ❀ *Keplerova 6 • Map A2 • 224 302430 •* **KKKKK**

2 Peklo
Continental dining in a grotto beneath Strahov Monastery. The house speciality, the "stuffed devil's hoof", is worth ordering. ❀ *Strahovské nadvoří 1 • Map A3 • 220 516652 •* **KKKKK**

3 Satay
A small restaurant serving Indonesian fast food. The limited menu can be tailored to suit vegetarians' needs. ❀ *Pohořelec 3 • Map A3 • 220 514552 • No credit cards •* **K**

4 Malý Buddha
The "Little Buddha" serves a wide range of potent teas and Vietnamese food. No smoking. ❀ *Úvoz 46 • Map B2 • 220 513894 • No credit cards •* **K**

5 U ševce Matouše
"At the Cobbler Matouš" has made an art of melting cheese on beefsteaks. The low, vaulted room is cosy. ❀ *Loretánské náměstí 4 • Map A2 • 220 514536 •* **KKK**

6 Lví dvůr
The rooftop dining room affords incomparable views of St Vitus; the beer-hall serves a sublime suckling pig. ❀ *U Prašného mostu 6 • Map B1 • 224 372361 •* **KKKK**

7 U Zlaté hrušky
"At the Golden Pear" serves delicious Continental and Czech game dishes in picturesque Nový Svět. ❀ *Nový Svět 3 • Map A2 • 220 514778 •* **KKK**

8 Restaurant u Lorety
A simple but reliable Czech eatery with aspirations to be something grander. Sit outdoors for a lunchtime serenade from the Loreto carillon. ❀ *Loretánské náměstí 8 • Map A2 • 220 517369 •* **KK**

9 Restaurant nad Úvozem
Meat-and-potatoes dining with sweeping views of Petřín Hill and Malá Strana. Accessed by a particularly steep and narrow staircase. ❀ *Loretánská 15 • Map B2 • No phone •* **KK**

10 Cowboys
The marvellous views from the roof-top terrace outdo the culinary aspects of this chic dinner club. Dine on the restaurant's enjoyable steaks and seafood against a lavishly eccentric decor. ❀ *Nerudova 40 • Map C2 • 800 152672 •* **KKKK**

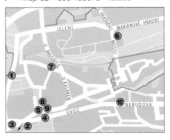

Left **Façade detail, Spanish Synagogue** Right **Vaulting, Pinkas Synagogue**

Josefov

IT IS IMPOSSIBLE TO DATE PRECISELY THE JEWS' ARRIVAL IN PRAGUE, *but historical sources mention the destruction of a Jewish settlement on the Vltava's left bank in the 13th century. For the next 500 years, Prague's Jews were obliged to live in a walled community where the Josefov quarter is today, working, studying and worshipping in the confines of the ghetto. So restricted was their allotted space that they were obliged to bury their dead layer upon layer in the Old Jewish Cemetery. When Emperor Josef II removed these strictures, many Jews left the ghetto, which became a slum occupied by the city's poorest residents. The quarter was razed in the late 19th century, making way for avenues such as Pařížská with its fine Art Nouveau houses. During World War II, the synagogues stored valuables looted from Jewish communities across the Reich – nearly 80,000 Czech and Moravian Jews perished in the Holocaust (see p25).*

🔟 Sights

1. Old Jewish Cemetery
2. Old-New Synagogue
3. St Agnes's Convent
4. Jewish Town Hall
5. High Synagogue
6. Maisel Synagogue
7. Ceremonial Hall
8. Klausen Synagogue
9. Pinkas Synagogue
10. Spanish Synagogue

Torah shield, High Synagogue

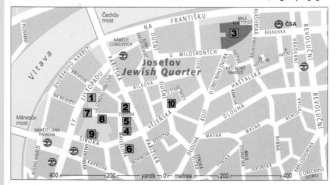

Sign up for DK's email newsletter on traveldk.com

Old Jewish Cemetery

and chapels. The artworks here, as part of the gallery's collection, comprise some of the best 14th-century Czech art (see pp28–9).

Jewish Town Hall
The hands of the town hall's Rococo clock turn backwards, as the Hebrew letters on its face are read from right to left. The building was one of Mordecai Maisel's gifts to his community in the late 16th century (see p35), but it was renovated in Baroque style in 1763. Ⓢ Maiselova 18 • Map L3 • Closed to the public

Old Jewish Cemetery
The sight of hundreds of graves, their leaning headstones crumbling on top of each other, is a moving and unforgettable experience – a testament to the treatment of the Jews in Prague, confined to their own ghetto even in death. Although there is no definite record of the number of burial sites here, to appreciate the depth of the graveyard, compare the gravestones' height with that of the street level on U Starého hřbitova (see pp22–3).

Old-New Synagogue
Attached to the Old Jewish Cemetery, Europe's oldest surviving synagogue has witnessed a turbulent history, including pogroms and fire, and has often been a place of refuge for the city's beleaguered Jewish community. Its name derives from the fact that another synagogue was built after this one, taking the title "new", but this was later destroyed. It is still the religious centre for Prague's small, present-day Jewish community (see pp24–5).

St Agnes's Convent
This lovely Gothic convent, now part of the National Gallery, is full of spectacular altarpieces and wall panels, as well as original 13th-century cloisters

High Synagogue
Constructed along with the town hall with funds from Mordecai Maisel, the High Synagogue was built in elegant Renaissance fashion. Subsequent reconstructions updated the exterior, but the interior retains its original stucco vaults. Inside there are also impressive Torah scrolls and mantles. Ⓢ Maiselova 18 • Map L3 • Closed to the public

Jewish Town Hall

Rabbi Loew

One of Prague's most famed residents, Rabbi Loew ben Bezalel (1512–1609) is associated with numerous local legends but he was also a pioneering pedagogue and a leading Hebrew scholar of the times. Foremost among the myths surrounding Loew is that of the Golem, a clay automaton the rabbi supposedly created to defend the ghetto *(see p52)*.

Maisel Synagogue

Rudolf II gave Mordecai Maisel permission to build his private synagogue here in the late 16th century, in gratitude for the Jewish mayor's financial help in Bohemia's war against the Turks. At the time of its construction it was the largest synagogue in Prague, until fire destroyed it and much of the ghetto in 1869. It was later rebuilt in Neo-Gothic style. Inside is a wonderful collection of Jewish silverwork and other items such as candlesticks and ceramics, much of it looted by the Nazis from other synagogues across Bohemia. Ironically, the Third

Ceremonial Hall

Reich planned to build a museum in Prague, dedicated to the Jews as an "extinct race". *Maiselova 10 • Map L3 • Open Apr–Oct: 9am–6pm Sun–Fri; Nov–Mar: 9am–4:30pm • Adm*

Ceremonial Hall

Built in the early 1900s in mock Romanesque fashion, the Ceremonial Hall was home to the Jewish community's Burial Society. The exhibits inside detail the complex Jewish rituals for preparing the dead for the grave. *U Starého hřbitova • Map K2 • Open Apr–Oct: 9am–6pm Sun–Fri; Nov–Mar: 9am–4:30pm • Adm*

Klausen Synagogue

Abutting the Old Jewish Cemetery, this Baroque single-nave building was constructed in 1694 on site of a school and prayer hall *(klausen)* where Rabbi Loew taught the *cabala*. Like most of the synagogues in the area, it is now houses Jewish exhibitions, including prints and manuscripts. *U Starého hřbitova 1 • Map K2 • Open Apr–Oct: 9am–6pm Sun–Fri; Nov–Mar: 9am–4:30pm • Adm*

Maisel Synagogue

Pinkas Synagogue

After World War II, this 15th-century building became a monument to the estimated 80,000 Czech and Moravian victims of the Holocaust – the names and dates of all those known to have perished either in the Terezín concentration camp or other extermination camps across Eastern Europe are written on the wall as a moving memorial. Equally moving is the exhibition of writings and paintings done by the children confined in Terezín. The Communists shut it down for "restoration" following the Six Day War in Israel in 1967. It was finally reopened in 1991. Ⓢ *Široká 3 • Map K3 • Open Apr–Oct: 9am–6pm Sun–Fri; Nov–Mar: 9am–4:30pm • Adm*

Spanish Synagogue

The opulent Moorish interior with its swirling arabesques and stucco decoration gives this late 19th-century synagogue its name. It stands on the site of a building known as the Old School, Prague's first Jewish house of worship. František Škroup, composer of the Czech national anthem, was the organist here in the mid-19th century. Ⓢ *Vézeňská 1 • Map M2 • Open Apr–Oct: 9am–6pm Sun–Fri; Nov–Mar: 9am–4:30pm • Adm*

Alms box, Klausen Synagogue

A Day in the Jewish Quarter

Morning

A sobering place to start the day, to appreciate how large the Czech Jewish community once was, is the **Pinkas Synagogue**, where Holocaust victims are listed by their home village and name. Then take a stroll through the adjoining **Old Jewish Cemetery** *(see pp22–3)*, where a guide will help you find significant gravesites. To lighten the mood, proceed to the **Klausen Synagogue** on the right, with its exhibits on Jewish festivals and family life.

At the end of U Starého hřbitova is the **Old-New Synagogue** *(see pp24–5)*, where you'll find treasures like Rabbi Loew's seat. Exiting, note the **Jewish Town Hall** *(see p99)* next door with its Hebrew clock. Just a few feet away, treat yourself to lunch at **Pravda** *(see p103)*.

Afternoon

After lunch, meander among the antiques shops en route to the **Maisel Synagogue**, where you'll find the first part of an exhibit on Jewish settlement in Bohemia and Moravia – it continues at the **Spanish Synagogue**.

Refresh yourself at **Bakeshop Praha** *(see p102)* around the corner before ending your tour at **St Agnes's Convent** *(see pp28–9)* with its exhibits of Czech medieval art.

A truly Josefov-style evening involves a kosher dinner at **King Solomon** *(see p103)* and a concert of sacred music at the Spanish Synagogue.

Left **Le Patio** Right **Pastries, Bakeshop Praha**

Top 10 Shops

1 Spanish Synagogue Gift Shop
Exquisite torah pointers, *yarmulkas* (skull caps) and other unique gifts, such as a watch in the style of the clock on the Jewish Town Hall *(see p99).*
◈ *Vězeňská 1 • Map L2*

2 Le Patio
This Pařížská shop sells unique home furnishings, and pieces made of glass, iron, leather and porcelain. Two other Prague locations, at Národní 22 and V Celnici 4, also have cafés.
◈ *Pařížská 20 • Map L2*

3 Michal Negrin
At this one-stop shop for all that glitters, you'll find baubles of amber, garnet and diamond from Fabergé and Swarovski jewellers. ◈ *Pařížská 7 • Map L2*

4 Precious Legacy
In addition to booking tours of Jewish sites in Prague and around Bohemia, Precious Legacy sells a tasteful range of prayer shawls, lamps, glass and... golems, golems, golems.
◈ *Široká 9 • Map L3*

5 Národní banka vín
Wine investors can sample the National Wine Bank's offerings before deciding whether to take a bottle home or leave it in a rented space in the cellar. Enquire about the next *dégustation* party. ◈ *Platnéřská 4 • Map K4*

6 Philharmonia
Take home your night at the opera. Philharmonia stocks the entire Czech musical canon, with recordings of contemporary Czech classical artists and the repertoires of the State Opera.
◈ *Pařížská 13 • Map L2*

7 Bakeshop Praha
Grab a bag of *rugalach*, brownies or other mouth-watering treats for on-the-go nourishment, or lunch on an egg-salad sandwich and coffee. Salads and quiches also to take away. ◈ *Kozí 1 • Map M1*

8 Antique Kaprova
This serious collector's shop specializes in prints and small decorative items such as clocks and lamps. If you don't find what you're looking for, just ask and they'll point you in the right direction. ◈ *Kaprova 12 • Map K3*

9 Jewish Art Gallery
Art lovers should peruse this small gallery's sale exhibition of local art. The original oils and sketches capture Josefov's bittersweet warmth and humanity. ◈ *Maiselova 9 • Map L3*

10 Alma Mahler Antique
What don't they sell? Alma Mahler Antique is a bazaar stocked with Persian rugs, jewellery, Meissen porcelain, crystal and nesting dolls. One of the largest antiques dealers in Prague. ◈ *Valentinská 7 • Map K3*

Price Categories

For a three-course meal for one with half a bottle of wine (or equivalent meal), taxes and extra charges.

K	under Kč300
KK	Kč300–Kč500
KKK	Kč500–Kč700
KKKK	Kč700–Kč1000
KKKKK	over Kč1000

Above **Café Franz Kafka**

🔟 Cafés and Restaurants

1 Café Franz Kafka
Dark wooden fixtures and black-tie service give this café a distinguished, Old World atmosphere. Take time out from sightseeing for a good café Vienna and apple strudel. Ⓢ *Široká 12 • Map L3 • 222 318945 • No credit cards •* **K**

2 Paneria
Pick up ready-made sandwiches for a picnic on the steps of the nearby Rudolfinum *(see p36)*. You'll find branches of Paneria at locations throughout the city. Ⓢ *Kaprova 3 • Map K3 • No credit cards •* **K**

3 Les Moules
This Belgian beer café offers typical brasserie cuisine along with a variety of shellfish dishes. A good selection of French cheeses is also on offer. Ⓢ *Pařížská Třída 19 • Map L2 • 222 315022 • Dis. access •* **KK**

4 Le Café Colonial
Enjoy an *espresso* and croissant in the stylish bistro for a snack or sit down to a marvellous French dinner in the dining room proper. Ⓢ *Široká 6 • Map L3 • 224 818322 •* **KKKK**

5 La Bodeguta del Medio
This Cuban-Creole restaurant offers grilled fish and meats using authentic ingredients. Popular with the business crowd, it boasts a great atmosphere and welcoming staff. Ⓢ *Kaprova 5 • Map K3 • 224 813922 • Dis. access •* **KKK**

6 King Solomon
Prague's foremost kosher restaurant has separate facilities for meat and dairy dishes. Closes for Friday sabbath. Ⓢ *Široká 8 • Map L3 • 224 818752 •* **K**

7 Siam-I-San (Arzenal)
Fiery curries and other Thai specialities. Ⓢ *Valentinská 11 • Map K3 • 224 814099 •* **KKKK**

8 Barock
Barock is the place to see and be seen, with its metal bar and floor-to-ceiling windows. Prague's elite come here to sample the excellent cocktails. Ⓢ *Pařížská 24 • Map L2 • 222 329221 •* **KK**

9 Modrá Zahrada
Usually crowded with people enjoying the large, thin-crust pizzas. Ⓢ *Pařížská 14 • Map L2 • 222 327171 •* **K**

10 Pravda
Fusion cuisine here is combined with a cool ambience. Popular with the upper crust, so book ahead. Ⓢ *Pařížská 17 • Map L2 • 222 326203 • Dis. access •* **KKKKK**

Note: Unless otherwise stated, all restaurants accept credit cards and serve vegetarian meals

Left **Roof detail, New Town Hall** Right **National Theatre**

New Town

FOUNDED IN 1348, *New Town* (Nové Město) *is hardly new. Charles IV's urban development scheme imposed straight avenues on the settlements springing up outside the old city walls and added a fifth town to the constellation of Vyšehrad, Hradčany, Old Town and Malá Strana. Unlike the Old Town, New Town was a planned grid of streets and markets. The horse market became Wenceslas Square in the 19th century; the 14th-century cattle market, and Europe's largest square, took on Charles's name, becoming Karlovo Náměstí. The hay market, Senovážné náměstí, kept its title until the Communists changed it for a time to honour the Russian novelist Maxim Gorky. Since the Velvet Revolution was played out on Národní and Wenceslas Square, these and surrounding streets have been filled with exciting enterprises.*

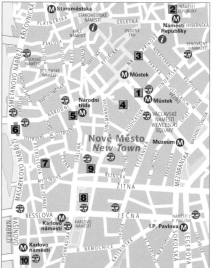

Statue, Franciscan Garden

Sights

1. Wenceslas Square
2. Náměstí Republiky
3. Na Příkopě
4. Franciscan Garden
5. Národní třída
6. National Theatre
7. The Globe Bookstore and Coffeehouse
8. Karlovo náměstí
9. New Town Hall
10. Palackého náměstí

Although some locals still call Senovážné náměstí "Gorkáč", it has returned to its old name on maps.

1 Wenceslas Square

This former horse market, in contrast to its medieval counterpart in the Old Town *(see pp14–17)*, expresses the history of 20th-century Prague, from its beautiful Art Nouveau façades to the memories of the many marches,

Na Příkopě

political protests and celebrations that have shaped the city over the past 100 years *(see pp30–31)*.

2 Náměstí Republiky

The odd couple of the Art Nouveau Municipal House and the Neo-Gothic Powder Tower are the centrepiece of Náměstí Republiky (Republic Square), facing the Czech National Bank's stern façade and the Hybernia Theatre, currently undergoing renovation. The composer Frédéric Chopin stayed briefly at a house that stood at the corner of Hybernská and Senovážná. Behind the theatre, at Hybernská 7, is the former home of the Lenin Museum, closed in 1991 after the Communists had lost power. The unassuming Church of St Joseph huddles in the northeast corner of the square. Map P3

Náměstí Republiky

3 Na Příkopě

Formerly a moat protecting the city's eastern flank, Na Příkopě is Prague's fashion boulevard, counting Benetton, Izod, Marks & Spencers and Taiza among its big-name stores. Shoppers jam the pedestrian zone and pavement cafés, streaming between the gleaming Myslbek Shopping Centre and Slovanský dům, with its 10-screen multiplex cinema. The Hussite firebrand Jan Želivský preached on the site now occupied by another shopping mall, the Černá Růže Palace. Map N5

4 Franciscan Garden

The Franciscans moved into this area near Wenceslas Square in 1603, reclaiming the former Carmelite monastery. The grounds and nearby Church of Our Lady of the Snow had fallen into decay following the Hussite civil war, but the monks beautifully restored them. The gardens remained closed to the public until 1950, when the Communists thought they were worth sharing. Although there's little love lost for the dictatorship of the proletariat, the gardens remain popular with young kissing couples and pigeon-feeding pensioners *(see p41)*. Map N6

Můstek

The area at the bottom of Wenceslas Square takes its name from the "Little Bridge" that spanned the moat here in medieval times. Below the surface, at the top of the escalators descending to the train platform, you'll find the remains of that bridge, uncovered by workers building the metro.

Karlovo náměstí

Národní třída

The end of Communism in Czechoslovakia began midway between the National Theatre and what is now the Tesco supermarket. On 17 November 1989, police put a brutal end to a pro-democracy march as it made its way to Wenceslas Square. A plaque under the arcade at Národní 20 marks where marchers and truncheons met. ◈ *Map L6*

National Theatre

Patriotic Czechs funded the theatre's construction twice: once in 1868 and again after fire destroyed the building in 1883. To see the stunning allegorical ceiling frescoes and Vojtěch Hynais' celebrated stage curtain,

take in one of the operas staged here; good picks are Smetana's *Libuše*, which debuted on this stage, or Dvořák's *The Devil and Kate*. Next door is Laterna Magika, where you can see black-light productions *(see p64)*. ◈ *Národní 2 • Map E4*

The Globe Bookstore and Coffeehouse

An expatriate institution, the English-language Globe moved here from its original home in 2000, leaving backpackers with outdated guidebooks stranded in Holešovice. The café is attracting a local following *(see p112)*. Chances are the people at the next table are eager to talk to you about their travels, for better or worse. ◈ *Pštrossova 6 • Map E5*

Karlovo náměstí

Charles IV had his city planners build New Town's central square to the same dimensions as Jerusalem's. Originally a cattle market, it's now a park popular with dog-walkers. Among the trees are monuments to such luminaries as Eliška Krásnohorská, who wrote libretti for Smetana's operas. To the west, on Resslova, is the Church of Sts Cyril and Methodius. The members of the Czech resistance, responsinble for the assassination of Nazi leader Reinhard Heydrich (1904–42), took refuge here *(see p39)*. ◈ *Map F5*

Auditorium, National Theatre

New Town Hall

9 In 1419, an anti-clerical mob led by Jan Želivský hurled the Catholic mayor and his councillors from a New Town Hall window in the first of Prague's defenestrations *(see p11)*. The Gothic tower on the building's eastern end was added a few years later; its viewing platform is open to the public. Crowds gather round the tower's base most Saturdays to congratulate newly-weds, married in the building's Gothic hall. ◎ *Karlovo náměstí 23 • Map F5 • Tower open May–Sep 10am–6pm Tue–Sun*

Palackého náměstí

10 The riverside square is named for the 19th-century historian František Palacký, whose work was integral to the National Revival. Stanislav Sucharda's sweeping monument to him stands at the plaza's northern end, while the modern steeples of the Emaus Monastery rise from the eastern edge. The church grounds are also known as the Slavonic Monastery, named after the liturgy the resident Balkan Benedictines used *(see p52)*. Sadly, American bombs demolished the monastery's original Baroque steeples on St Valentine's Day 1945, as part of the Allies' World War II military campaign. ◎ *Map E6*

Emaus Monastery, Palackého náměstí

A Day in New Town

Morning

🕐 Start your day with breakfast at **Hotel Evropa** *(see p112)*, then head to **Wenceslas Square** *(see pp30–31)* to begin the day's sightseeing. A quick peep inside the **National Museum** *(see p36)* will probably suffice unless it's raining or you're a big fan of natural history. From there, proceed to St Wenceslas's statue and the monument to Communism's victims, where you can pay tribute to the nation's growing pains.

Get in a bit of retail therapy along the square as you walk up to Můstek, then visit the **Museum of Communism** *(see p37)*, ironically located above McDonald's and a casino.

Take the metro to Národní třída, and linger over a book or newspaper at the **Globe** for a leisurely lunch.

Afternoon

After lunch, head up to the **National Theatre** and then follow the Vltava's Right Bank upstream to Jiráskovo náměstí. Modern-art buffs should take in **Galerie Mánes** *(see p110)* on the way. Follow Resslova up the hill to the **Church of Sts Cyril and Methodius** and its monument to Czechoslovak resistance fighters.

In the evening, take in a performance at the National Theatre; **Brasserie M** *(see p113)* is the obvious choice for dinner, before or after. If you still have the energy, head to **Radost** *(see p111)* to dance the night away or to **U Havrana** *(see p112)* for a local, smoky atmosphere.

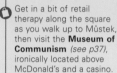

Left **Galerie Mánes** Right **Dvořák Museum**

🔟 Galleries and Museums

1 Galerie Mánes
Occupying the southern tip of Žofín Island, this contemporary art gallery hosts both Czech and foreign artists. ❧ *Masarykovo nábřeží 250 • Map E5 • Open 10am–6pm Tue–Sun • Adm*

2 Oskar Kokoschka Gallery
The gallery of the Austrian Cultural Institute highlights the shared cultural heritage of Prague and Vienna. Shows have included retrospectives of Oskar Kokoschka and Gustav Klimt.
❧ *Jungmannovo náměstí 18 • Map M6 • Open 10am–1pm, 2–4pm Mon–Fri • Adm*

3 Postage Stamp Museum
Philatelists' mouths water over this one. Its exhibitions illustrate the colourful history of postage stamps in the Czech Republic and Europe. Sells commemorative sheets and graphic works too. ❧ *Nové mlýny 2 • Map G4 • Open 9am–noon, 1–5pm Tue–Sun • Adm*

4 Museum of the City of Prague
Visitors can explore 19th-century Prague with Antonín Langweil's scaled replica of the city. ❧ *Na Poříčí 52 • Map P3 • Open 9am–6pm Tue–Sun • Adm*

5 Mucha Museum
Art Nouveau artist Alfons Mucha is a national hero. Here you'll find his journals, sketchbooks and paintings, both private and commercial. ❧ *Panská 7 • Map N5 • Open 10am–6pm daily • Adm*

6 Museum of Communism
A triptych of the dream, reality and nightmare that was Communist Czechoslovakia. To fill the museum, its creators combed the country for mementos of its totalitarian past *(see p37)*.

7 Wax Museum Praha
Madame Tussaud's, it isn't, but its collection includes the best – and likely only – waxwork representations of President Václav Havel, tennis star Martina Navrátilová and author Franz Kafka *(see p50)*.

8 National Museum
Palaeontology, mineralogy and a host of other "ologies". The museum's collections are scattered throughout the country, but the Wenceslas Square edifice is a cultural artifact in its own right *(see p36)*. ❧ *Václavské náměstí 68 • Map G5 • Open Oct–Apr: 9am–5pm daily; May–Sep 10am–6pm (closed first Tue of month) • Adm*

9 Police Museum
The museum documents the police's efforts with engaging exhibits, such as an interactive crime scene. ❧ *Ke Karlovu 1 • Map G6 • Open 10am–5pm Tue–Sun • Adm*

10 Dvořák Museum
This Baroque palace houses the 19th-century composer's piano and viola, as well as other memorabilia of his life and work *(see p45)*. ❧ *Ke Karlovu 20 • Map G6 • Open 10am–5pm Tue–Sun • Adm*

Left **Radost** Right **Jazz Café č. 14**

🔟 Nightspots

1 Radost
Late at night, club kids take over the disco, lounge and café. By day, a broader demographic comes for the good vegetarian food. Sunday brunch is especially popular. Open until 5am *(see p66)*. ✆ Bělehradská 120 • Map G6

2 Zvonařka
Tucked into a residential neighbourhood is one of the city's less hectic nightspots. Good food and drink. Summer guests can enjoy the view from the large patio. ✆ Šafaříkova 1 • Map H6

3 Akropolis
Tons of amazing international acts have played here. A popular music venue with Prague locals, you can catch a touring band one night and a local singer the next. ✆ Kubelíkova 27

4 Lucerna
The granddaddy of Prague's clubs, the cavernous Lucerna hosts live jazz as well as rock and dance parties, including the ever popular Eighties night *(see p67)*.

5 N11
Billed as Prague's first New York nightclub, N11 combines a sleek discotheque with good pub-style dining. Open until the early hours of the morning. Strangely, journalists and medical staff receive a 10 per cent discount – the club's owner is both. ✆ Národní 11 • Map E5

6 Jazz Café č. 14
Popular with an artsy student crowd that seems determined to blot out the lamp light with cigarette smoke. Otherwise, a comfortable retreat for sipping coffee or cheap wine. ✆ Opatovická 14 • Map E5

7 Reduta Jazz Club
Celebrated musicians have played here including ex-US President Bill Clinton. Come here to hear all types of jazz from swing bands to modern styles. ✆ Národní 20 • Map L6

8 Café Louvre
Franz Kafka, Max Brod and their writer friends used to hold court here. It's a bright, cheerful place, good for conversation and a bite to eat. At the back is Prague's classiest pool hall. ✆ Národní 20 • Map L6

9 Ultramarin
The ground floor is a simple, convivial bar and restaurant. After you've had your fill, you'll find a music club downstairs, where you can dance. Open until 4am. ✆ Ostrovní 32 • Map E4

10 Billiard centrum v Cípu
Close to 100 billiard, pool and snooker tables, plus four lanes of bowling and two table-tennis sets. Don't go on Friday or Saturday without making a reservation first. The bar serves drinks, but no food. ✆ V Cípu 1 • Map P5

Left **The Globe Bookstore and Coffeehouse** Right **U Fleků**

Cafés and Pubs

1 The Globe Bookstore and Coffeehouse
The quality of the food varies with the Globe's mercurial staff, but the overall trend is upward. Weekend brunch is the best time to visit *(see p106)*.

2 Solidní Nejistota
The name is bigger than the café. Serves good coffee, homemade pastries and a dozen flavours of ice cream. ◊ *Pštrossova 21 • Map E5*

3 U Fleků
Exactly what you might expect from the city that created the "Beer-Barrel Polka". U Fleků is probably the city's most popular beer hall, and the prices reflect it *(see p60)*. ◊ *Křemencova 11 • Map E5*

4 Zlatá hvězda
This is a sports bar for serious fans. Watch sports on their multiple screens while dripping barbecue sauce down your front. ◊ *Ve Smečkách 12 • Map G5*

5 Jágr's
Owned by "friends and family" of National Hockey League star Jaromír Jágr, this sports bar has several giant screens, decent food and friendly service. ◊ *Václavské náměstí 56 • Map N6*

6 Gott Gallery
An excellent Art Nouveau style café. Enjoy good coffee while admiring the bold art on display. ◊ *Spálená 29 • Map F4 • 224 996775 • Dis. access • KK*

7 Rocky O'Reilly's
This lively pub offers all a Celtophile could ask for: live music in the evenings, football on the TV, a roaring fire and plenty of stout. The food's fair as well. ◊ *Štěpánská 32 • Map F5*

8 Shakespeare and Sons
Soak up the café's laidback vibe with English-language books and coffee. The owners have maintained a community feel, offering a variety of events and readings with Bernard beer on tap. ◊ *Krymská 12 • 271 740839 • Dis. access • K*

9 French Institute Café
Students at the Institut Français and other Francophones gather here for coffee, quiche and a read of the French newspapers. The garden is a peaceful spot on sunny days. ◊ *Štěpánská 35 • Map F5*

10 U Havrana
One of a dying breed, the Raven serves some of the best greasy food in town and a superior half-litre of beer. It is open until 5am. ◊ *Hálkova 6 • Map G5*

Recommend your favourite pub on traveldk.com

Price Categories

For a three-course meal for one with half a bottle of wine (or equivalent meal), taxes and extra charges.	**K** under Kč300
	KK Kč300–Kč500
	KKK Kč500–Kč700
	KKKK Kč700–Kč1000
	KKKKK over Kč1000

Above **Zahrada v opeře**

🔟 Restaurants

1 Dynamo
This postmodern diner serves dishes such as marinated tongue in black sauce and liver and onions. A wide selection of single-malt scotches. ◎ *Pštrossova 29 • Map E5 • 224 932020* • **KK**

2 Tulip
Stylish and earthy, the café and wine bar serves American-style breakfasts all day and a wide selection of vegetarian dishes. ◎ *Opatovická 3 • Map E5 • 224 930019* • **KK**

3 Universal
A popular eatery, serving substantial meals at small prices. The café is especially recommended for its vegetarian dishes. ◎ *V Jirchářích • Map E4 • 224 934416 • Dis. access* • **KK**

4 Brasserie M
Only a handful of tables in this tiny French bistro, meaning attentive service and well-crafted dishes, prepared in an open-kitchen. Book ahead. ◎ *Vladislavova 17 • Map F4 • 224 054070* • **KK**

5 U Pinkasů
A great-value Czech beer hall since 1843, this is a very popular lunchtime destination. The food is simple but hearty, and the atmosphere lively. ◎ *Jungmannovo náměstí 16 • Map F4 • 221 111150* • **KK**

6 Buffalo Bill's
More Tex than Mex, Buffalo Bill's is a friendly saloon featuring good food, country music and accommodating staff. Colouring-book place-mats and specials for children. ◎ *Vodičkova 9 • Map F4 • 224 948624* • **KK**

7 Lemon Leaf
Serving Thai and Burmese specials, the ingredients used are fresh and the presentation is colourful. Service is fast and friendly. ◎ *Myslíkova 14 • Map E5 • 224 919056 • Dis. access* • **K**

8 Jama Restaurace
Jama offers delicious Tex-Mex and American specialities. It also has an internet café, video rental shop and an outdoor beer garden. ◎ *V jámě 7 • Map F4 • 224 222383* • **K**

9 Cicala
This authentic Italian eatery is a magnet for visiting film stars and the like. The fresh pasta can't be beat. ◎ *Žitná 43 • Map F5 • 222 210375 • No credit cards* • **KKKK**

10 Zahrada v opeře
The "Garden at the Opera" is the perfect gourmet dinner choice before or after a night at the State Opera. Outstanding value for money, too. ◎ *Legerova 75 • Map G6 • 224 239685* • **KKK**

Note: Unless otherwise stated, all restaurants accept credit cards and serve vegetarian meals

Left **Holešovice** Right **View of Prague from Smíchov**

Greater Prague

PRAGUE'S CITY CENTRE CAN KEEP MOST VISITORS *occupied for days, but if you're staying outside the city's heart, or if you have the time to explore beyond the capital's walls, the outlying areas offer plenty of surprises. Over the centuries, Prague's various rulers have used the surrounding countryside as their personal playground, building impressive castles, palaces and parks to which they could escape the often claustrophobic streets and winding alleyways of the city. Even the Communists have left their own kind of functional mark on the area, with somewhat ugly but useful towers and exhibition spaces. From the peaceful parklands of Vyšehrad or the social atmosphere of Letná, to the rowdy nightlife of Žižkov, to the intriguing gardens of Holešovice and Troja, Greater Prague has a diversity that will fulfil almost any requirements you might have.*

Troja Château

🔟 Sights

1. Vyšehrad
2. Smíchov
3. Vinohrady
4. Holešovice
5. Letná Park
6. Stromovka
7. Troja
8. Výstaviště
9. Monument of National Liberation
10. Žižkov TV Tower

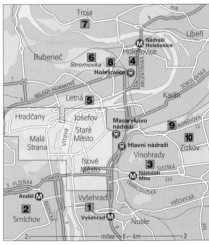

1 Vyšehrad
The former fortress of Vyšehrad *(see p121)* is steeped in legend. Bedřich Smetana paid tribute to the second seat of the Přemyslid dynasty that resided here in the 10th century in his opera *Libuše* and in his rousing patriotic work *Má vlast (see p44)*. The composer is buried here in the National Cemetery, as are many other luminaries of Czech culture. ◈ *Map B6*

Vinohrady

2 Smíchov
Today, modern shopping centres and multiplex cinemas have taken over what used to be the city's main industrial centre. At the heart of the district is Anděl metro station, which still bears traces of its Communist origins – the station was originally named "Moscow" and was decorated with Soviet murals *(see p49)*. ◈ *Map A6*

3 Vinohrady
Originally the royal vine-yards, Vinohrady today is a gently rolling residential neighbourhood. The central square, Náměstí Míru, features the Neo-Gothic Church of St Ludmila and the Art Nouveau Vinohrady Theatre. For a bit of peace and greenery visit the botanical gardens. ◈ *Map B6*

4 Holešovice
Developers are helping this former warehouse district make a comeback. It's home to the National Gallery's Veletržní Palace *(see pp26–7)*, and motor car fans will love the National Technical Museum, with its exhibits of Czech interwar vehicles such as Škodas. ◈ *Map B5 • National Technical Museum: Kostelní; Open 9am–5pm Tue–Sun; Adm • Dis. access*

5 Letná Park
A grand staircase leads from the Vltava riverbank opposite the Josefov quarter *(see pp98–103)* to a giant metronome. The needle marks time where a mammoth statue of Joseph Stalin once stood before it was demolished in the 1960s *(see p48)*. The surrounding park echoes with the clatter of skateboards and barking dogs. Travelling circuses sometimes set up in the open fields, but Letná's popular beer garden is probably its biggest draw. ◈ *Map E1*

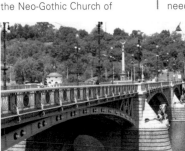
Letná Park

Žižkov

This working-class neighbourhood came into being when city fathers divided the expanding Královské Vinohrady district. The inhabitants of the area thumbed their noses at Habsburg rule and named their new district after the Hussite warrior. Žižkovites' contrary nature runs deep, even having a separatist movement which promotes an independent Republic of Žižkov. An alternative culture thrives around the Akropolis club and the Divus artists collective, and increasingly, numerous ethnic restaurants are bringing an international touch to the area.

Stromovka

King Otakar established the royal game park here in the 13th century; it's been a public garden since 1804 (stromovka means "place of trees"). Stroll, skate or simply enjoy the ancient trees by day and visit the planetarium by night. The fish ponds were a creation of Rudolf II – the emperor drilled a tunnel under Letná to bring in water to supply them (see p41). ◉ Map B5

Troja

The riverside gardens and chateau of Troja are an excellent destination for a day trip out of the city. Cross the Vltava from Stromovka, take in the château's beautiful garden and art collection (see p120), the Baroque chapel of St Clare and the zoological gardens. There is a bus from here that will take you back to the centre. ◉ Map B5

Výstaviště

The fair grounds here were originally built at the end of the 19th century to host trade shows, but nowadays you're more likely to see a hockey match or a rock concert at Paegas Arena, or a Shakespeare performance at a replica of London's Globe Theatre. There's an amusement park with rides for the kids, an outdoor cinema and the oddly charming musical Křižík Fountain (see p51). If you want to see the original statues that graced Charles Bridge, rather than today's replicas, pay a visit to the Lapidárium, where they are preserved (see p120). ◉ Map B5

Monument of National Liberation

View of the Žižkov Tower

9 Monument of National Liberation

The one-eyed Hussite general Jan Žižka defeated invading crusaders in 1420 atop the hill where his giant equestrian statue now stands in front of the Tomb of the Unknown Soldier. Erected in 1929, the monument serves as a memorial to all those who suffered in the Czech struggle for independence. The Communists co-opted the building, and for a time it served as President Klement Gottwald's mausoleum (see p48). ◈ Žižkov • Map B6 • Open Sep–Jun: first Sat of month

10 Žižkov TV Tower

The Communists unashamedly cleared away a Jewish cemetery on the site in the 1970s to make way for this eyesore, reaching almost 100-m (300-ft) in height. However it didn't begin transmitting until after the Velvet Revolution. Despite a viewing platform, the tower is actually too tall to see anything clearly, but thrill-seekers may want to try. ◈ Mahlerovy sady • Map B6 • Dis. access • Adm

Three Afternoons in Greater Prague

Afternoon One

See **Vyšehrad** (see p115) late in the day, but only if the weather looks promising. Take the metro to the Vyšehrad stop at the Congress Centre, from which you have marvellous views of Prague's spires. Walk west along Na Bučance and enter the fortifications through the **Tábor Gate** (see p121). Once inside the walls, you'll find historic constructions, such as the Romanesque **St Martin's Rotunda** (see p121), everywhere you turn. Enjoy the park at your leisure but get to the westernmost edge of the compound atop Vyšehrad's rocky outcrop in time for a sunset.

Afternoon Two

Žižkov and **Vinohrady** (see p115) are also best seen in the second half of the day. From Florenc metro, climb to the **Monument of National Liberation** for a wonderful view, then compare it to the one you get from the **Žižkov TV Tower**. Stroll as far into Vinohrady as your feet will permit you, but save your strength: you'll need it for a night of pubbing and clubbing.

Afternoon Three

Energetic walkers can see **Stromovka** and **Troja** in a half-day. Take the tram to **Výstaviště** among the trees of the former game park before crossing the Vltava to the **Troja Château** (see p120). From there, you're within easy walking distance of the zoo. Take the bus back to the metro at Nádražì Holešovice.

Following pages Troja Château

117

Left **Troja Chateau** Centre **Bertramka** Right **Olšany Cemetery**

Best of the Rest

1 Lapidarium
This is where Prague's statues go when they retire. Among the 700-plus items is the original St Wenceslas from Wenceslas Square. ◎ *Výstaviště 422, Holešovice • Map B5 • Open noon–6pm Tue–Fri; 10am–6pm Sat–Sun • Dis. access • Adm*

2 Troja Château
Jean-Baptiste Mathey created Count Sternberg's 17th-century palace when Classical Italian was the rage. It has a collection of 19th-century Czech art. ◎ *U Trojského zámku 1, Troja • Map B5 • Open Apr–Oct: 10am–6pm Tue–Sun; Nov–Mar: 10am–5pm Sat–Sun • Adm*

3 Troja Zoo
Prague's zoological gardens, date back to 1924. The most popular exhibits are the big cats and gorillas. ◎ *U Trojského zámku 120, Troja • Map B5 • Zoo: Jun–Aug 9am–7pm; Apr, May, Oct 9am–6pm; Nov–Feb 9am–4pm; Mar 9am–5pm • Adm*

4 Břevnov Monastery
St Adalbert founded this Benedictine monastery in 993. You can see remains of the Romanesque church, and the 18th-century church of St Margaret. ◎ *Markétská, Břevnov • Map B5 • 220 406111 • Guided visits (in Czech): Apr–Oct: 10am, 2 & 4pm Sat & Sun; Nov–Mar: 10am & 2pm Sat & Sun • Adm*

5 Bertramka
The house where Mozart and his wife stayed while the composer worked on *Don Giovanni* has been turned into a small museum on his life. ◎ *Mozartova 169, Smíchov • Map A6 • Open 9:30am–6pm Tue–Sun (till 4pm Nov–Mar) • Adm*

6 Barrandov Studios
The Nazis turned Prague's film studios into a propaganda mill during World War II, as did the Communists, but today they are thriving as western filmmakers discover Prague *(see pp46–7)*. ◎ *Kříženeckého náměstí 5, Barrandov • Map B5 • 267 071111 • Open by appt • Free*

7 Olšany Cemetery
Plague victims were interred here when the site was still far from the city. Notable residents include Jan Palach, a student who burned himself alive in protest at the 1968 Warsaw-Pact invasion. ◎ *Map B5*

8 New Jewish Cemetery
The writer Franz Kafka's memorial is here, as are those of many other Prague Jews who perished in the Holocaust *(see p25)*. ◎ *Map B5*

9 Slapy Reservoir
The dam in the Vltava not only helps prevent flooding, it makes a nice swimming and boating reserve. ◎ *Map B5*

10 Panelaks
The majority of Prague's residents still live in these avowedly ugly prefab estates. Have a look around and consider yourself lucky. ◎ *Map B5*

Don't miss the chairlift ride over the whole complex of Troja Zoo – great for kids.

Left **Church of Sts Peter and Paul** Right **Rotunda of St Martin**

🔟 Vyšehrad Sights

1 Church of Sts Peter and Paul
The first church to stand on this site was founded by Vratislav II in the 11th century, but the Neo-Gothic structure seen today dates from 1885. The altar is decorated with a beautiful Gothic panel depicting *Our Lady of the Rains*. 🛇 *K Rotundě • Metro Vyšehrad • Open May–Nov: 10am–noon, 1–4pm Mon, Wed, Thu, Sat & Sun; 10am–noon Fri*

2 Slavín Monument
The burial place of notable Czech cultural figures, students laid flowers in remembrance here on 17 November 1989, before marching into town for the Velvet Revolution *(see p35)*. 🛇 *K Rotundě • Metro Vyšehrad • Open 8am–5pm daily*

3 Devil's Pillar
The story goes that the devil bet a local priest that he could carry this pillar to St Peter's Basilica in Rome before the clergyman finished his sermon. A sore loser, he threw the column to the ground here. 🛇 *K Rotundě • Metro Vyšehrad*

4 Casements
In the 18th century, occupying French troops drilled holes in Vyšehrad rock to store ammunition. 🛇 *Metro Vyšehrad*

5 Rotunda of St Martin
This 11th-century chapel is the oldest in Prague and most likely to be the oldest Christian house of worship in the country. It was reconstructed in 1878. 🛇 *K Rotundě • Metro Vyšehrad*

6 Tábor Gate
Charles IV restored Vyšehrad's fortifications in the 14th century. Catholic crusaders rode through this gate on their way to crush the Táborites in 1434. 🛇 *Na Bučance • Metro Vyšehrad*

7 Congress Centre
The Communist Palace of Culture is trying hard to make up for its ugliness by hosting pop concerts and international conferences. 🛇 *Metro Vyšehrad*

8 Nusle Bridge
As charmless as the Congress Centre, this viaduct spans the Nusle Valley, connecting New Town to the Pankrác banking and commercial district. 🛇 *Metro Vyšehrad*

9 Cubist Houses
Cubist architecture took off in Prague, as a cluster of houses below Vyšehrad testifies. Josef Chochol built the angular buildings on Podolské nábřeží, Libušina and the corner of Přemyslova and Neklanova. 🛇 *Metro Vyšehrad*

10 Smetana's Grave
At the start of each year's Prague Spring music festival *(see p68)*, musicians attend a ceremony at composer Bedřich Smetana's grave. 🛇 *Metro Vyšehrad*

Left **Hlučná samota** Right **U Vystřeleného Oka**

Cafés and Pubs

1 La Creperie
This French-owned café does a solid business of crêpes, waffles and other Gallic delicacies. A nice selection of French and other imported wines, too. ◈ *Janovského 4, Holešovice • Map B5*

2 U Vystřeleného oka
The name "At the Shot-Out Eye" is a tribute to the half-blind Hussite general Jan Žižka from whom Žižkov takes its name and whose enormous statue looms overhead *(see p117)*. ◈ *U Božích bojovníké 3, Žižkov • Map B6*

3 U Holanů
Tuck into a plate of pickled sausages or herring at Vinohrady's favourite no-nonsense pub. Simple but clean, with perfunctory service; they don't make them like this anymore. ◈ *Londýnská 10, Vinohrady • Map B6*

4 Meduza
The junk-shop setting has been a favourite of neighbourhood hipsters and students for years. It's an excellent spot to spend a rainy afternoon sipping tea or Moravian wine. ◈ *Belgická 17, Vinohrady • Map B6*

5 Hospůdka nad Viktorkou
Bořivojova street boasts more pubs per metre than any other place in the country, and possibly the world. There's nothing elegant about nad Viktorkou, but it's the ultimate Prague pub. ◈ *Bořivojova 79, Žižkov • Map B6*

6 Potrefená husa
"The Wounded Goose," as Potrefená husa translates as, is the place to go to watch football over fish and chips. Several domestic and imported beers are available for a loud and lively clientele. ◈ *Resslova 1 • Map E5*

7 Pastička
"The Mousetrap" is a perfect blend of old-fashioned beer hall and modish gastro-pub. Visit it for a choice of light and dark Bernard beer and good, filling food. ◈ *Blanická 25, Vinohrady • Map B6*

8 Café Faux Pas
Start the day at this café which opens at 8am, serving a variety of sweet and savoury *crêpes* and fresh sandwiches. ◈ *Vinohradská 31 • Map H5*

9 Hlučná samota
This refined pub takes its name from Bohumil Hrabal's novel *Too Loud a Solitude (see p45)*. Neither loud nor solitary, guests return time and again for the excellent beer and food. ◈ *Zahřebská 14, Vinohrady • Map B6*

10 Hapu
Working-class Žižkov might not be the first place you'd look for excellent daiquiris, martinis and gin fizzes, but sink into a sofa, order from a choice and enjoy. Warning: the room is tiny and fills up fast. ◈ *Orlická 8, Žižkov • Map B6*

Price Categories

For a three-course meal for one with half a bottle of wine (or equivalent meal), taxes and extra charges.

K	under Kč300
KK	Kč300–Kč500
KKK	Kč500–Kč700
KKKK	Kč700–Kč1000
KKKKK	over Kč1000

Above **Il Ritrovo**

🔟 Restaurants

1 Il Ritrovo
Some of the best pasta in town is hiding out at this family-run spaghetteria. Any of the fresh pastas are worth your while. ◈ *Lublaňská 11, Vinohrady • Map B6 • 224 261475 • Dis. access •* **KK**

2 Olympos
Prague's best Greek food. The large garden, complete with table tennis, is ideal for summer dining. The mixed salad platter is the best value around. ◈ *Kubelíkova 9, Žižkov • Map B6 • 222 722239 • Dis. access •* **KK**

3 Mailsi
This little Pakistani eatery offers better value than the Indian restaurants in the centre. Close to the No. 9 tram stop, it's not as remote as it appears. ◈ *Lipanská 1, Žižkov • Map B6 • 222 717783 • No credit cards •* **KK**

4 Rana
When Mehfooz Ahmed sold Mailsi to his brother, his fans followed him here, where he serves up the best curries in town. The vindaloo is for true spice devotees. ◈ *Na Dědince 12, Palmovka • 721 809084 • No credit cards • Dis. access •* **K**

5 Hanil
A selection of Japanese and Korean dishes. If you're desperately seeking sushi, make this your destination. ◈ *Slavíkova 24, Žižkov • Map B6 • 222 715867 • No credit cards • Dis. access •* **KK**

6 Hotel Diana
It's a trek getting here, but Hotel Diana wins the prize for the best game restaurant. The dill-and-potato *kulajda* soup is a must. Try the boar, too. ◈ *Hůrská 12, Prague 14 • 266 610060 •* **KK**

7 Restaurant Voyta
The Hotel Voyta's elegant in-house restaurant is something of a local culinary secret. Have the venison Wellington under the ancient chestnut trees and you'll see why many would like it to stay that way. ◈ *K Novému dvoru 124, Prague 4 • 261 711307 •* **KKKK**

8 U Cedru
Here's where insiders go for an authentic Lebanese dining experience. Order a large spread of hummus, tabbouleh and other appetizers with pitta. ◈ *Národní Obrany 27, Dejvice • 233 342974 •* **KKK**

9 Ambiente
Steaks, salads, ribs and other American dishes keep tables full – reservations a must. The menu changes regularly, but they'll never part with the chocolate fondue. ◈ *Mánesova 59, Vinohrady • Map B6 • 222 727851 •* **KK**

🔟 Rudý Baron
In this Red Baron-themed restaurant the menu maintains an American focus, with a few European touches, such as beef-steak with truffles. ◈ *Korunní 23, Vinohrady • Map B6 • 222 514485 • Dis. access •* **KK**

Note: *Unless otherwise stated, all restaurants accept credit cards and serve vegetarian meals*

STREETSMART

PRAGUE'S TOP 10

Left **Ruzyně Airport** Right **Hlavní Nádraží central station**

🔟 Getting to Prague

1 By Air
More than 40 international airlines fly to Prague's Ruzyně airport. The national carrier Czech Airlines (ČSA) is a member of the Sky Team alliance, whose members include Delta, Air France and Alitalia. Direct flights from London are about 1.5 hours; from New York, about 9 hours. ⊗ *ČSA: 239 007007 • www.csa.cz*

2 Ruzyně Airport
Located 15 km (9 miles) northwest of the city centre, Ruzyně is Prague's only international airport. Until 1989, a cheery, red neon hammer-and-sickle greeted visitors landing here. There are all the modern facilities here now, though, including car rental offices, bureaux de change, shops and restaurants. Municipal buses serve the airport, as does a reputable private transport service, but their cars charge more than taxis do.

3 By Train
Prague is on major European rail routes; the Orient Express's London–Paris–Venice route passes through town. International trains to the Czech capital are comfortable, with couchette sleeping facilities, and fast excepting delays at the border, and a cheap alternative to flying if you have time.

4 By Coach
Coaches are your best bet for long journeys on a budget. But these buses are often crowded and uncomfortable. Two metros and several trams stop at Prague's main bus terminal Florenc.

5 By Car
If you're going to be driving in the Czech Republic for more than 30 days, you'll need an international driver's licence. If you bring your own car, you must carry a vehicle registration card and a red warning triangle, and display a national identification sticker. A major motorway connects Prague to the Slovak capital of Bratislava; otherwise, it's all A and B roads.

6 Customs
Visitors from outside the EU can bring goods worth less than 175 euros (about Kč5,000) into the country without paying a duty. Two litres or less of wine, one litre of spirits and 200 cigarettes (or their equivalent in tobacco) can also be brought in duty-free.

7 Discount Deals
Travellers from London should check with easyJet or SmartWings for return tickets to Prague at reasonable prices. If you can be flexible about when you travel, look for stand-by tickets from Airhitch.

⊗ *Airhitch: www.airhitch. org • easyJet: www. easyjet.com • SmartWings: www.smartwings.net*

8 Visas and Passports
Most visitors may stay visa-free in the Czech Republic for up to 90 days, but it is always wise to confirm this with the Czech embassy in your own country or your travel agent for up-to-date visa requirements. Czech immigration officials may request you to be carrying at least Kč1,100 per day for your visit (or have a valid credit card).

9 When to Go
While there's no bad time to visit, Prague, like most European capitals, is teeming with tourists during the summer months. Off-season rates for hotels are usually in effect from September to March; check when making your booking. Winter is cold but beautiful under snow.

10 Long Stays
If you choose to stay longer than 90 days, you'll need to apply for a long-term visa, valid for a year. For this, you'll need proof of employment, health insurance and housing as well as a clean criminal record. This visa can be renewed annually for eight years, after which you can apply for permanent residency.

Left **Prague metro station** Right **Prague bus**

🔟 Getting Around Prague

1 Metro
Prague's underground transit system is fast, efficient and, with a little practice, easy to navigate. There are three lines, known as A, B and C; or more commonly, red, yellow and green. Validate your ticket, available from vending machines at the stations' vestibules, at the ticket barriers. These passes are valid for all Prague public transport.

2 Tram
Prague trams make it easy to see much of the city while saving you shoe leather. The schedules can be a little tricky to read, however, and re-routings are frequent. Buy tickets in advance – they are available all over the city from newsagents, and from metro stations.

3 Buses
Buses serve outlying areas – they are banned from the centre because of pollution. As with trams, riders must validate their tickets by using the punching machines on the bus. For some stops, riders must notify the driver of their intention to get off by pressing a button near the door.

4 Taxis
Prague's taxis have received a lot of bad press (see p129), but most firms are now reliable. Phone a central despatcher in advance – your hotel will be able to give you a number – to be assured of safety and a fair price. If the car doesn't have a lighted sign with the word "taxi" written on it, don't get in. And make sure the meter's running. Generally, avoid taxis that line up outside the major tourist sights.

5 Driving
Prague's city centre was not designed for the volume of traffic it sees nowadays. The streets are narrow and winding and parking is very scarce. If you must drive, keep to the right, wear a seatbelt, and be aware that traffic violations are payable on the spot. Illegally parked cars are regularly clamped or towed away by viligant traffic wardens.

6 On Foot
Walking is the only way to see much of the city. The centre is only about 4 km (2.5 miles) from end to end and many of the historic sights, such as Prague Castle (see pp8–11) and the Old Town Square (see pp14–17) are in pedestrianized zones. Make sure you wear comfortable, flat-soled shoes, watch your step on the cobblestones, and look out for trams that drive in the centre of the road in both directions.

7 River Boats
A river cruise along the Vltava can offer a relaxing and romantic afternoon of sightseeing that's easy on weary feet. Tour boats depart from Čechův and Palackého bridges. You can also rent rowing boats near Charles Bridge.

8 Horse and Carriage
Horse and carriages line Old Town Square and take tourists for short rides through the surrounding streets. This can make a pleasant (and romantic) after-dinner diversion. Surprisingly, the horses don't seem to mind the crowds and auto traffic.

9 Cycling
While Prague has numerous bicycle routes, cyclists do not have their own lanes on the streets and must share the road with cars, which can prove hazardous. The cobblestones can also be hard going. Some services offer guided cycling tours of the city – check with the Prague Information Service (see p128).

10 Guided Tours
While some guided tours are little more than a mob following a distant umbrella, many services offer personal insight to the city. Check with the Prague Information Service, or look for posters advertising pub crawls.

Left **The Prague Post** Right **Prague Information Service office**

☰10 Sources of Information

1 Prague Information Service

The Prague Information Service (PIS) serves as a central clearing house for information about all kinds of concerts, theatre performances and other cultural events. They literally have it all, from discos to art galleries, and publish it in a monthly guide available at their offices around town and on the Internet. They will also supply you with useful maps, and all the staff are English-speaking.
⊗ Prague Information Service: Staroměstské náměstí 1 & Main station Hlavní nádraží • 12 444 • www.pis.cz

2 Čedok

The state-run tourist office has locations all over the city and can offer the usual advice required by tourists, such as hotel accommodation, cultural events and details of guided tours, both in Prague and outside the city. They have a lot of English-language material to hand out for free.
⊗ Čedok: Na příkopě 18 • 224 187777 • www. cedok.cz

3 The Prague Post

Don't listen to the jaded expatriates, who take pleasure in bringing this long-standing newspaper down. This English-language weekly has been publishing a fair

semblance of news for more than 10 years. The entertainment, cinema, exhibition and restaurant guides are well-nigh essential. There are also interesting articles on local politics and events. It is available from most newsstands.

4 Internet

A quick search for "Prague" on any search engine will give you links to hundreds of web sites catering to Bohemians and bohemians alike. These offer a variety of information about where to stay, weather reports, hotel accommodation, travel and much more.

5 Radio Prague

Conveniently located at the same frequency as the BBC (101.1 FM), Radio Prague is the foreign-language service of state-run Czech Radio. It broadcasts morning and evening summaries of local and international news in English, plus other insightful features.

6 Kulturní Přehled

The preferred publication of the Czech reader has got it all. Two hundred or so pages published every month list all theatres, concerts and clubs, as well as current exhibitions in museums and galleries. It is also useful if you want to find out what's playing at the nearest cinema.

7 Houser.cz

One of many counter-culture magazines on sale in the city, this free publication has been covering the city's club scene for more than five years. Although it's not necessarily credible, it's still entertaining. Definitely one for the twenty-something visitors to Prague who want to know about current nightlife.

8 Prague Tribune

An English-language trade and lifestyle monthly for the business professional is also of interest to tourists for its smart interviews with movers and shakers and fun reviews.

9 In Your Pocket

This monthly mini-magazine is your one stop travel and information publication. A perfect resource to finding the best hotel or restaurant and also to find out what the city has to offer. Contains travel advice and tips. Available at newsstands across the city.

10 Prahabulletinboard

An eccentric gentleman named "Uncle Curt" distributes announcements, invitations and calls for help, as well as the occasional anti-globalization rant in this free email service, read by local residents and visitors alike.

Left **Crowds on Charles Bridge** Right **Taxis lined up at tourist sight**

Streetsmart

🔟 Things to Avoid

1 Midday on Charles Bridge
Unless you enjoy being packed cheek-to-jowl with fellow travellers, visit this popular spot *(see pp18–19)* sometime other than midday. The mobs start arriving around 10am, especially during summer. Early risers can have the bridge more or less to themselves at sunrise.

2 Pickpockets
Tourists are an easy target for petty thievery. Avoid any place where you'll be pressed up against strangers. Pickpockets on trams and metro cars have numerous routines to relieve travellers of their valuables. Have a copy of your passport and avoid carrying too much cash.

3 Unscrupulous Taxi Drivers
The best way to avoid being taken for a ride, as it were, is to phone a central despatcher *(see p127)* to send a car to you. Avoid using cars marked "transport", and those without pricing information posted on the door and never agree to "negotiate" a price – taxis should always have a meter running.

4 Two-Tiered Pricing
While it violates the law to charge tourists more, many reputable establishments, including the Jewish Museum *(see p99)*, offer a 50 per cent discount to Czechs. Simply letting ticket sellers know you're aware of the lower price helps, but it is still no real guarantee that you won't be penalized for being a foreigner.

5 Re-routed Trams
In a city as old as Prague, the infrastructure needs constant repair. This means tearing up streets and, inevitably, re-routing your tram. *The Prague Post* contains a weekly list of route and schedule changes, so check here before setting off. To avoid confusion, timetables for re-routed trams are yellow instead of white.

6 Dog Mess
The municipal authorities gave up many years ago trying to count how many canine residents Prague has. It has also largely absolved itself of trying to clean up after them. Local dog-owners are also notoriously careless, so watch your step.

7 Prostitution
Despite the best intentions of the law, the oldest profession still thrives in a "grey zone" of the city. Never assume that prostitution is legal. Even saints should avoid prostitutes of both sexes: they are often known to supplement their incomes by picking pockets.

8 Non-Stop and Herna bars
Unfortunately, Prague has too few reputable bars and cafés open into the early hours. The words "non-stop" and *"herna"* are synonymous with shady characters; the latter are filled with slot machines and gambling addicts. You'd be better off getting an early night, or paying to get in to a nightclub.

9 Skinheads
Owing to 40 years of Communist isolation, some Czechs are sadly unaccustomed to people who do not look like them, or dress like them. Since 1989, the Neo-Nazi skinhead movement has grown at a disturbing rate. Random, unprovoked violence against dark-skinned individuals is not uncommon, but it is unlikely to affect you in the main tourist areas.

10 Food Poisoning
Cases of lethal food poisoning are very rare, but mild cases are common; be familiar with the symptoms, such as nausea and diarrhoea. Stands selling food on the street are more likely to cause problems than proper restaurants, as the ingredients are exposed to bacteria and often not very well cooked. When in doubt, avoid fish, eggs and products including mayonnaise.

Left **Prague pensione** Right **The Globe Bookstore**

TOP 10 Accommodation Tips

1 Off-season Prices
The peak tourist season runs roughly from April through to September with another pocket of high prices around New Year; check whether prices have been hiked up for a particular event before booking. Recently an accommodation company has started offering last-minute prices for numerous hotels; you can check their availability at www.accomgroup.com.

2 Bargain Districts
Exploring accommodation options outside the city centre can save you a considerable amount on your hotel bills. The neighbourhoods of Žižkov, Karlín, Smíchov and Holešovice, for example, all have good connections to the centre *(see pp114–17)* and an increasing number of good quality hotels.

3 Annonce
If you're staying a bit longer than the average tourist and want to save money on long-term accommodation, check the daily classified advertisement publication *Annonce*. Almost all the ads are in Czech, but if you can find someone to translate, you'll find affordable rooms and apartments for rent, both on short- and long-term agreements. *Annonce* is available from most newsagents.

4 Hotel Standards
If you recognize the name of your hotel (such as a chain hotel), you'll recognize the quality of the services and amenities; otherwise, be prepared for surprises. Not all hotel rooms have en suite bathrooms, for example, or plush bath towels. If such items are important to you, enquire before you book.

5 Things to Avoid
If you've failed to book a room in advance, go directly to a local travel agent or hotel. Do not accept accommodation from touts at the airport, train station or bus depot. Even if they're not out to rob you, you have no guarantee as to the quality of the rooms.

6 Parking
Smaller hotels may not have reserved parking spaces for guests. If so, ask the management about the safest places to park. Never leave valuables in your car and make sure you're parked in a legal space; being towed or clamped can ruin precious holiday time.

7 Pets
Prague is a very pet-friendly city – good news for animal-owners and bad news for allergy sufferers. When you book, check whether you can bring pets; if you fear the fur, ask for assurances that your room hasn't been doubling up as a kennel recently.

8 Security
Whatever the destination, it almost goes without saying that tourists should use common sense when it comes to travelling with valuables – if possible, leave anything you wouldn't want to lose at home. In the better hotels, keep items such as passports and jewellery in the hotel safe. Be aware that even the best hotels can be targets of streetside scams.

9 Short-term Apartment Rentals
If you're staying a week or longer, you may want to skip the hotels entirely and rent a small flat. The Prague Information Service, state travel agency Čedok and numerous other local agencies can help you find a short-term rental *(see p128)*.

10 Finding a Flat
Many real estate companies offer sublets, long-term and month-to-month rentals. For a fee, usually the value of one month's rent, they can find you a home and help you with the necessary paperwork. If you want to go it on your own, check bulletin boards at The Globe Bookstore *(see p106)*.

Left **Vegetarian snack** Right **Prague café**

🔟 Eating and Drinking Tips

1 Vegetarian Tips
Meat- and dairy-free dining is no longer the problem it was a few years ago. Many new restaurants, such as Dahab, offer vegetarians a wide variety of tasty meatless meals, while older establishments are increasingly sensitive to vegetarians' needs. That said, never assume your vegetables won't come smothered with cheese. ⊗ *Dahab: Dlouhá 33 • Map M2 • 224 827375 • **KK***

2 Ordering
Except for the grander eateries, many Prague restaurants have yet to grasp multiple-course service. Emphasize that you want your appetizer *(jako předkrm)* before your main course. You will probably also have to order your side dish *à la carte*. Your steak will be well-done unless you plead otherwise.

3 Paying
Verify the restaurant takes credit cards before you order. Restaurants seldom accept travellers' cheques. Tell your waiter you'd like to pay with one word: *zaplatím*. You and your party may pay *dohromady* (all together) or *zvlášť* (separately).

4 Tipping
While tipping in Prague is approaching the international standard of 15 per cent, it is still common in pubs to simply round up the bill. If your beer and schnitzel cost Kč82, for example, pay Kč90. Rather than leaving the tip on the table, tell your waiter how much you want to give.

5 Making Reservations
Reserving a table is never a bad idea and can save you a great deal of hungry wandering come dinner time. In many restaurants, it's common for lone diners to join other tables. If you're alone and want to know if a seat is free, point at it and ask *"Je tu volno?"*

6 Smoking
Prague restaurants are seldom non-smoking. A local ordinance bans smoking at lunch time, but it is seldom, if ever, enforced. For a smoke-free meal, try the vegetarian restaurants Country Life and Little Buddha. ⊗ *Country Life: Melantrichova 15; Map L4; 224 213366; **K**; and Jungmannova 1; Map M6; 257 044419; **K** • Little Buddha: Úvoz 46; Map A3; 220 513894; **K***

7 Late-Night Eating
Unless you're willing to hazard the sausage stands on Wenceslas Square, finding a bite late at night will prove challenging. The club Radost *(see p111)* serves food until the early hours. Better hotels have late-night room service.

8 Breakfast
Your hotel will probably include a Continental breakfast with the price of your room. While Irish fry-ups can be found at bars such as the James Joyce and Caffrey's, American diner-style breakfasts are largely unheard of. Cafés increasingly serve *hemenex* – ham and eggs – but seldom open before 9am. ⊗ *James Joyce: Liliová 10; Map K5; 224 248793; **K** • Caffrey's: Staroměstské náměstí 10; Map M3; 224 828031; **K***

9 Brunch
If you're travelling on a budget but still want a taste of the good life, you can see how the other half eat without breaking the bank by doing brunch at one of the city's fine-dining establishments. Brunch buffets, complete with champagne and jazz, abound and seldom cost more than Kč600.

10 Restaurant Classes
State-licensed eating establishments fall into one of three classes, with first class being the finest and three the plainest. The restaurant's class should be posted by the front door. These classifications are no indications of quality. A first-class pub may very well offer better food than a first-class restaurant at times.

For a guide to restaurant prices See p79

Left **Antiques shop** Right **Second-hand bookshop**

TOP 10 Shopping Tips

Credit Cards
1 The more expensive the item, the more likely it will be that you can pay for it with a credit card. Shops selling souvenirs are more likely to accept credit cards than those selling necessities. Cards accepted by an establishment will be indicated on the shop's front door.

VAT Refunds
2 Tourists are entitled to a refund of the value-added tax on purchases. Ask for a tax-free shopping cheque and tax-free envelope at the store. Complete the cheque and have it stamped at customs within 30 days. In Prague, visitors can collect their refund at several shops at Ruzyně airport *(see p126)*.

Baskets and Bags
3 If there are shopping carts or baskets at the front of the store, take one as you go in. It's common courtesy – shopkeepers will assume you're a shoplifter without one – and it helps regulate the number of shoppers in the often tiny stores. Bags for your purchases may cost extra.

Small Change
4 Prague tellers demonstrate a disturbing antipathy towards mathematics and always appreciate it if you have exact change, down to the last heller. Don't be surprised if the clerk fishes the correct coins out of your hand. Smaller shops may even refuse to accept banknotes larger than Kč1,000.

Specialist Shops
5 Large department stores such as Tesco and Carrefour have now introduced one-stop shopping, but there is still the tendency in Prague for shops to specialize to an amusing degree. A *papírnictví* sells everything made of paper, from notepads to sanitary napkins, while the only place you'll find an alarm clock is at a *hodinářství*.

Bargain Food
6 Whole loaves of fresh sourdough bread go for less than Kč20. But be warned – this bread is free of preservatives, so it starts to go off after a day. Shops selling *grilované kuře* (roast chicken) are dotted around the city. Order a quarter or half bird to eat there, or, if you are in self-catering accommodation, you can take a whole bird home for a great dinner.

Fresh Vegetables
7 Large supermarkets often trade in quality for quantity when it comes to produce. The best fruit and vegetables are found at various outdoor markets around Prague. In the city centre, try Havelská.

Antiques
8 Antiques dealers and junk merchants abound in the city centre. Going further afield will offer you an even better selection and prices. You may need a special permit to export antiques from the Czech Republic; ask the dealer. If you're looking for Soviet paraphernalia, be warned that anything you find these days is likely to be a replica.

Books
9 If you're looking for some reading material for the next leg of your journey, head to Anagram, Big Ben or The Globe bookstore *(see p106)*, but don't expect the latest titles. Or try Czech booksellers such as Kanzelsberger, where English-language classics go for a song.
⊗ Anagram: Týn 4, Map M3 • Big Ben: Malá Štupartská 5; Map M3 • Kanzelsberger: Václavské náměstí 4; Map N5

Bootleg Goods
10 As with most major cities, the odds are very good that the Adidas trainers, Calvin Klein underwear or Umbro sportswear that you can buy on street stalls is not the real thing. Also be aware that many bazaars sell pirated CDs, videos and software, so the quality is likely to be dubious, if not downright unuseable.

Establishments that accept credit cards most commonly accept Visa, MasterCard and American Express.

Left **Museum tickets** Right **Guru nightclub**

TOP10 Prague on a Budget

1 City Public Transport

You can buy 24-hour, 3-day and 7-day passes valid for unlimited use on Prague's metro, trams and buses. Validate the ticket once and enjoy the ride, but don't forget to sign the back: an unsigned ticket is not valid and ticket inspectors that appear unexpectedly can levy a fine up to Kč950.

2 Opera

Prague opera continues to defy the laws of supply and demand. Even the best seats are cheap by western standards, but it's possible to buy standing-room only tickets and then slip into a seat in the largely empty hall when the overture begins.

3 Concerts

Corporate and state sponsorship keeps ticket prices – and musicians' salaries – low for the city's major orchestras. The Czech Radio Orchestra, Prague Symphony Orchestra and other ensembles regularly give masterful performances, the tickets to which are seldom more than a few hundred crowns.

4 Beer

There's seldom any need to pay more than Kč30 for a half-litre of draft beer. Even within the centre, Kč20 beer is not uncommon. Or journey out to Žižkov (see p116) or other working-class neighbourhoods as cheap as Kč12.

5 Food

Even less expensive than pub fare is the food served cafeteria-style at the city's many lunch counters and buffets. Grab a tray, your Czech dictionary and join the queue. Food is usually sold by weight. Lunch, with beer, should be less than Kč150.

6 Accommodation

Hostels usually have small double and even single rooms that offer greater privacy (see p144). Travellers can also find rooms or even entire flats for rent by the week (see p146). Check the bulletin boards at The Globe Bookstore (see p106) and Radost nightclub (see p111).

7 Travel in the Czech Republic

Students and teachers qualify for discounts on bus and train tickets, as well as airfares offered by GTS International. Czech trains have first- and second-class cabins, the latter being the cheaper. You can travel to most destinations within the Czech Republic and back for less than Kč400.
⊗ GTS International: Ve Smečkách 33; Map G5; 257 187100 • www.gtsint.cz

8 Unofficial Tours

If you don't care for leading yourself around the city, try asking a student hanging around Café Konvikt (see p78) or elsewhere to show you around; you get an insider's view of the sights, while the student gets a welcome free English lesson. An additional plus is that you will see much of Prague Castle without paying admission.

9 Clubbing

While admission to Karlovy Lázně, Radost and Roxy will cost you Kč200 or more at weekends, even these big clubs have free nights during the week. Smaller clubs further afield, such as Akropolis, Guru and Industry 55, are cheaper and more intimate but a little less polished (see pp66–7).

10 Museums

Admission to National Gallery art exhibits at various venues around town is typically low, but not as low as the entrance to the National Museum (see p36). Natural history buffs will be delighted here as well as at the Municipal Museum. The many exhibitions at the National Technical Museum (see p115) outside the centre are far more interesting than the functional name might initially suggest.

Left **Náměstí Republiky, starting point for guided bus tours** Right **Wallenstein Garden**

TOP 10 Prague for the Disabled

Public Transport
Prague has only recently begun to think about the transportation needs of the disabled. Many of the newer metro stations have lifts and auditory beacons for the blind, but older stations in the centre remain largely inaccessible. Most wheelchairs won't fit in the city's trams and the city's cobbled streets can be hard-going.

Barrier-Free Prague'
This free brochure outlines four sightseeing routes, with easy-to-read maps and brief informative texts, for wheelchair-users. The guide also lists barrier-free galleries, monuments, restaurants, public bathrooms and shops along the route. Pick it up at the Prague Association of Wheelchair Users.

Prague Association of Wheelchair-Users
In addition to publishing the above brochure, this group lobbies for the rights of the disabled. You can pick up the brochure and get advice about various other disability issues at their office near Náměstí Republiky. Some of their staff speak English.
◈ *Prague Association of Wheelchair Users: Benediktská 6 • Map N2 • 224 827210 • www.pov.cz.*

Bus Routes
Prague has only two buses dedicated to wheelchair-users. Carrying passengers from far-flung housing developments to a few central locations, they're not much use to tourists. Many other buses have low platforms, but again, they mainly serve outlying areas.

Bus Tours
Those visitors who have trouble walking can get an overview of the city by taking an open-topped bus tour around town. Pre-recorded narration in several languages plays during the trip. Look for the buses on Old Town Square *(see pp14–17)* and Náměstí Republiky.

Accessible Sights
As may now be clear, Prague isn't the most disabled-friendly of the world's capital cities. The following sights are at least partly accessible to wheelchair-users, although getting to them is sometimes a problem: St Vitus's Cathedral *(see pp12–13)*, the Old Royal Palace *(see pp8–11)*, the Old Town Hall *(see pp16–17)*, the National Theatre *(see p64)*, Wallenstein Garden *(see p40)*, Franciscan Garden *(see p105)*, the Municipal House *(see p72)*, the Church of St James *(see p74)* and the Estates Theatre *(see p65)*.

Discounted Tickets
Hearing impaired visitors will be happy to learn that most sights offer discounted entry.

Hotels
Most of the newer hotels are accessible to wheelchair-users, although the number of barrier-free rooms is small. Hats off to the Hilton, where there are no fewer than 15 barrier-free rooms *(see p139)*. The Prague Association of Wheelchair-Users will also be able to supply a list of accessible places to stay.

Helper Dogs
Canine assistants to the visually impaired are permitted in banks, official buildings and historic monuments as well as on public transport. Be aware that not all members of Prague's thriving dog population are as well-trained – avoiding dog mess is a problem for the sighted too.

Other Resources
Other organizations in the city that are a good source of information for disabled travellers are listed below.
◈ *Czech Union of the Deaf: Havlíčkova 4; Map G2; 224 816559 • United Organization of the Blind and Visually Impaired: Krakovská 21; Map G5; 221 462146; www.braillnet.cz*

Left **Goethe Institute** Right **Charles University**

🔟 Studying in Prague

Czech Lessons
Large language schools like Berlitz offer Czech lessons for foreigners, as does Charles University. Absolute beginners can take an intensive, four-week course for less than Kč5,000. 🄯 *Berlitz: SF Servis • Náměstí Jana Palacha 2 • Map K3 • 222 319645 • http://ubs.ff.cuni.cz*

Goethe Institute
Accomplished German speakers can study Kafka in the original language; the rest can brush up their language skills or start from scratch. A five-month course in conversational German costs Kč4,000. 🄯 *Goethe-Institut Prag: Masarykovo nabřeži 32 • Map E5 • 221 962111 • www.goethe.de/ms/pra*

French Institute
English may have replaced it as the lingua franca, so to speak, but French is still useful for travellers. Four-month courses for beginners cost around Kč4,000. You can also study French art, history, literature – even creative writing. 🄯 *Institut Francais de Prague: Štepánská 35 • Map F5 • 222 232995 • www.ifp.cz*

Anglo-American College
This liberal arts college offers internationally accredited degrees in business administration, political science and legal studies, as well as programmes in journalism and Eastern European studies. All courses are taught in English. 🄯 *Anglo-American College: Lázeňská 4 • Map D3 • 257 530202 • www.aac.edu.*

Charles University
The oldest university in Central Europe offers some courses in English in its many degree and non-degree programmes. Short-term courses are taught over the summer months. 🄯 *Univerzita Karlova v Praze: Ovocný trh 5 • Map N4 • 224 491111 • www.cuni.cz.*

New York University
New York University offers study-abroad programmes for students enrolled at its US campuses and at affiliated universities elsewhere. Students enrolled in Czech universities may audit classes. 🄯 *New York University in Prague: Malé náměstí 2 • Map L4 • 224 226658 • www.nyu.cz.*

Prague Centre for Further Education
Established in 1995, the Prague Centre organizes courses on a wide range of subjects such as information technology, Czech history, and fashion design. Six-week courses cost Kč4,000 (with discounts for students, teachers and groups) and are offered frequently throughout the year. 🄯 *Prague Centre for Further Education: Karmelitská 18 • Map C3 • 257 534013 • www.prague-center.cz*

International TEFL Certificate
This private firm has been training its students all over the world for six years to teach English to foreigners. Courses last four weeks. ITC assists graduates in job placement worldwide. 🄯 *www.itc-training.com*

English-Language Grammar Schools
Expat parents can enroll their children at the International School of Prague, Riverside School and other grammar schools offering English-language instruction for children aged 3-18. 🄯 *International School of Prague: www.isp.cz • Riverside School: www.riversideschool.cz*

Driving Lessons
Long-term residents will need to apply for a Czech driving licence. Some driving schools such as Autoškola Ing. Ondšej Horázny and Autoškola Dejvice offer instruction and testing in English. See the Prague *Yellow Pages* for a more complete list. 🄯 *Autoškola Dejvice: www.autoskola dejvice.cz • Autoškola Ing. Ondřej Horázny: www. horazny.cz*

Left **Prague bank** Centre **Bureau de Change sign** Right **Post Office sign**

10 Banking and Communications

1 Currency
The Czech Republic's currency is the crown (Kč), which is made up of 100 hellers. Crown notes come in denominations of Kč5,000, Kč2,000, Kč1,000, Kč500, Kč200, Kč100, Kč50 and the increasingly rare Kč20. Coins come in the following denominations: Kč1, Kč2, Kč5, Kč10, Kč20 and Kč50, as well as 50 hellers.

2 Banks
Most banks are open from 8am to 5pm. Although some banks, such as Živnostenská banka, are worth visiting just for their stunning interiors, the only other reason you'll need to go to a Prague bank is if you want to take advantage of the typically lower fees they charge for currency exchange.
§ *Živnostenská banka: Na Příkopé 20 • Map P4*

3 Exchange
Although they may advertise "0 percent commission", all bureaux de change will take a cut. The conversion rates vary little from exchange to exchange so there's little point shopping around. Note that very few will accept coins. It's a good idea to convert your crowns back to your own currency before you leave, as the Czech currency has a very low value outside of the country itself.

4 ATMs
Bankomats are widely available throughout the city centre, although they are out of order *(mimo provoz)* with alarming frequency. The machines that *are* working recognize major credit cards and global banking systems such as Cirrus. Be vigilant when using ATMs after dark.

5 Credit Cards and Travellers' Cheques
Major credit cards are widely accepted at shops and restaurants that cater to tourists, but always check on your way in. Travellers' cheques, on the other hand, are seldom accepted, although American Express cashes and sells their cheques at their various offices.

6 Telephones
When not out of order, payphones accept either coins or phone cards *(telefonní karty)*, available at post offices and newsagents. More than 70 per cent of Czechs have mobile phones. You can rent a mobile phone at Prague's Ruzyně airport *(see p126)*.

7 Post
The main post office is lovely inside and worth a visit, whether or not you need to mail a postcard or letter overseas. It also offers a telegram service and a large phone room, which is a good way of making overseas telephone calls. Main Post Office:
§ *Jindřišská 14 • Map P6 • 221 131111*

8 Internet
As in most cities, nowadays one can find an Internet café on almost every corner. Expect to be charged upwards of Kč60 an hour, with a minimum time of 15 minutes. Many visitors do their surfing at The Globe. § *The Globe: Pštrossova 6 • Map E5 • 224 916264*

9 Newspapers and Magazines
In addition to the locally produced *Prague Tribune* and *The Prague Post (see p128)*, downtown newsstands carry US weeklies like *Time* as well as international newspapers such as *The Guardian*, *Wall Street Journal* and the *International Herald Tribune*.

10 Television and Radio
You'll find some English-language broadcasts on the BBC at 101.1 FM, as well as an abundance of Czech and Slovak. If your hotel has satellite hook-ups, expect the usual fare of Sky and MTV. Public Czech Television often broadcasts classic films in English with Czech subtitles.

Left **Prague ambulance** Centre **Police sign** Right **Pharmacy sign**

🔟 Security and Health

1 Emergency Numbers

To call an ambulance, dial 155; for police, 158. In the event of a fire, call 150. Speak slowly and calmly and the operator will understand you. For an English-speaking emergency operator, dial 112. You may also wish to carry your embassy's phone number with you.

2 Police

Prague's municipal police are generally helpful to (law-abiding) visitors, although they continue to be dogged with accusations of bribe-taking. Don't confuse members of private security services and Prague Castle guards for state or municipal police officers.

3 Hospitals

Prague's doctors increasingly speak English and are accustomed to western standards of care. Some private clinics that cater to foreigners, such as the Canadian Medical Centre, have doctors on call 24 hours a day. Should you need in-patient care, go to the foreigners' clinic at Na Homolce Hospital. 🕲 *Canadian Medical Centre: Veleslavínská 1; 235 360133 • Na Homolce Hospital: Roentgenova 2; 257 272146*

4 Fire

If you need to report a fire, dial 150 and tell the operator what is burning and where. In the street, it's not uncommon to see a smouldering waste bin, where someone has carelessly thrown a lit cigarette. Don't worry – someone will be along in a minute with a bucket of water to put it out.

5 Dentists

Czech dental care is considered among the best in Europe. For dental emergencies, call 22494 6981. For routine care, try the English-speaking dentists at the American Dental Associates or Millennium Dental Care. 🕲 *American Dental Associates: V Celnicí 4; 221 181121 • Millennium Dental Care: V Celnicí 10; 221 033405; info@mdc.cz*

6 Pharmacies

For even such common medicines as aspirin or cold remedies, you'll need to visit a *lékárna*. A pharmacy at the Kotva department store is open at weekends, but most are closed. There are 24 other pharmacies scattered around the city and a 24-hour pharmacy at Palackého. 🕲 *24-hour pharmacy: Palackého 5; 224 946982 • Štefanikova 6*

7 Precautions

Consult a physician before your trip and check whether your health insurance covers you abroad. If it doesn't be sure to take out extra insurance to avoid high charges should you fall ill. Also be aware that your medication may be known by a different name brand abroad. Your doctor may also recommend an inoculation against hepatitis before your trip, although this isn't strictly necessary.

8 Pickpockets

Pickpockets target tourists in crowded spaces where they can jostle you. Distribute your valuables among several inside pockets and never carry more cash than you need. Leave photocopies of your passport in your hotel room.

9 Food and Water Safety

The fat-heavy Czech diet may cause indigestion, so bring along your favourite stomach-settler. Tap water is safe to drink, but even local residents prefer bottled water. The most dangerous fluid in a city full of bars is alcohol; watch your intake – Czech beer is stronger than a lot of other varieties.

10 Smoking

Second-hand smoke is a fact of life in Prague. Smoke-free restaurants and cafés are rare. If cigarettes aggravate your health or enjoyment, be sure to visit in summer, when you can spend more time outside and breathe in fresher air.

Left **Hotel Hoffmeister** Right **Hotel Paříž**

🔟 Luxury Hotels

1 Hotel Hoffmeister

The Hoffmeister is a quiet, modern hotel in the shadow of Prague Castle, celebrated for its gourmet restaurant and gallery of caricatures by the owner's father. The rooms are sumptuously and uniquely furnished. ⊗ *Pod Bruskou 7 • Map D1 • 251 017111 • www. hoffmeister.cz • Dis. access • KKKKK*

2 U Zlaté studně

Once owned by astronomer Tycho de Brahe, the hotel "at the Golden Well" adjoins the Ledeburg Gardens, offering unparalled views. All rooms have whirlpool baths and Richelieu furniture. Book well in advance. ⊗ *U Zlaté studně 4 • Map C2 • 257 011213 • www.zlatastudna.cz • No air conditioning • KKKKK*

3 Hotel U krále Karla

Formerly a Benedictine monastery, the King Charles Hotel was popular in the 16th century for the reputed healing powers of its well. The hotel is a blissful matrimony of Baroque furnishings and modern luxuries. ⊗ *Úvoz 4 • Map B2 • 257 533594 • ukralekarla@romantic hotels.cz • No air conditioning • KKKKK*

4 Hotel Pod věží

The "Hotel Under the Tower" guards the Malá Strana end of Charles Bridge. The rooms are graciously outfitted with period furniture and comfortable reproductions. Hair-stylists, barbers, manicurists and masseuses are on call. ⊗ *Mostecká 2 • Map D3 • 257 532041 • www.podvezi.com • KKKKK*

5 Four Seasons

Swaddled in the Four Seasons trademark luxury, guests may forget where they are. A quick stroll on the riverside terrace should remind them. The restaurant Allegro is one of Prague's best. Top-notch, all around. ⊗ *Veleslavínova 2a • Map K3 • 221 427000 • www.fourseasons.com • Dis. access • KKKKK*

6 Grand Hotel Bohemia

Old European decorum meets Old European decadence: built in 1920, the Bohemia was home to one of Jazz-Age Prague's liveliest clubs. Its 78 rooms were refurbished in 2002. The best views are from the eighth floor. ⊗ *Králodvorská 4 • Map P3 • 234 608111 • www.grandhotelbohemia. cz • Dis. access • KKKKK*

7 Dům u Karlova mostu

Also known by its address Na Kampě 15, the "House at Charles Bridge" is close enough to the river that guests can hear the Vltava rushing over the weir. The rooms and suites are warmly furnished in a country style. ⊗ *Na Kampě 15 • Map D3 • 257 531430 • www. archibald.cz • No air conditioning • KKKK*

8 Mandarin Oriental

The hotel is located in a restored Dominican monastery. Its spa is in the former chapel and several of its 99 rooms have views over the city to Prague castle. ⊗ *Nebovidská 1 • Map C3 • 233 088888 • www.mandarinoriental. com/prague • KKKK*

9 Hotel Paříž

Built in 1904, this Art Nouveau treasure retains all its original charm while incorporating modern conveniences like heated bathroom floors and king-size beds in all rooms. The Royal Tower Suite has a 360-degree view. ⊗ *U Obecního domu • Map P3 • 222 195195 • www.hotel-pariz.cz • KKKKK*

10 Pachtuv Palace

Rooms at the Pachtuv Palace are luxuriously over the top, with painted ceilings and medieval decor, fittings and fixtures. Located on the waterfront, the views are spectacular. It is so romantic that it may be hard to leave your room. ⊗ *Karoliny Světlé 34 • Map K6 • 234 705155 • www. pachtuvpalace.com • KKKKK*

***Note:** Unless otherwise stated, all hotels accept credit cards, and have en-suite bathrooms and air conditioning*

Price Categories

For a standard, double room per night (with breakfast if included), taxes and extra charges.

K	under Kč1,500
KK	Kč1,500–Kč3,000
KKK	Kč3,000–Kč4,500
KKKK	Kč4,500–Kč6,000
KKKKK	over Kč6,000

Above **Holiday Inn**

🔟 Chain Hotels

1 Hotel Ibis
A no-nonsense hotel with modern amenities and a devotion to customer service. The rooms are small, clean and comfortable. A good choice for travellers who don't want to spend a lot of time sitting around. ◈ *Šaldova 54, Prague 8* • *222 332800* • *www.hotelibis.cz* • **KKK**

2 Novotel
With underground parking, a small gym and swimming pool, piano bar and Continental restaurant, the Novotel offers a budget version of luxury. Children under 16 stay free. ◈ *Kateřinská 38* • *221 104999* • *www.novotel.com* • *Dis. access* • **KKK**

3 Holiday Inn
The new hotel adjoining the Congress Centre near Vyšehrad was chosen as Best Hotel Project of 2001. Drivers will appreciate the large garage and adjoining petrol station. Ask for a castle view. ◈ *Na Pankráci 15* • *Map B6* • *296 895000* • *www.holidayinn.cz* • *Dis. access* • **KKKKK**

4 Hotel Meteor Plaza
Medieval travellers who found city gates closed for the night stayed at a much earlier hotel on this spot. The fitness centre on the premises has two whirlpool baths. For a longer stay, book room No. 510. ◈ *Hybernská 6* • *Map P4* • *224 192111* • *www.hotel-meteor.cz* • **KKKKK**

5 Prague Marriott
Bright and welcoming, with pleasant touches such as complimentary newspapers, signs in braille and rooms with lofts (great for families). All rooms have internet access and 24-hour room service. ◈ *V Celnici 8* • *Map G2* • *222 888888* • *www.marriott.com* • *Dis. access* • **KKKK**

6 Hilton
Prague's premiere convention hotel boasts nearly 800 rooms and suites, an extensive fitness centre, a casino and the largest meeting facilities aside from the Congress Centre in Vyšehrad. Rates go down in summer. ◈ *Pobřežní 1* • *Map H1* • *224 842458* • *www.hilton.com* • *Dis. access* • **KKKKK**

7 Prague Renaissance
Situated between Masarykovo nádraží and the Old Town, the Renaissance offers a fitness centre with pool, three restaurants, 314 rooms and 12 suites; all rooms have satellite TV and voice mail. ◈ *V Celnici 7* • *Map G2* • *221 821111* • *www.renaissancehotels.com* • *Dis. access* • **KKKK**

8 Kampa Hotel
Recently acquired by Best Western, the Kampa is a happy blend of the familiar standards and local peculiarity; the in-house restaurant takes the hotel's medieval arms-and-armour theme to a delightful extreme. The 84 rooms are smallish, but quite cosy. ◈ *Všehrdova 16* • *Map C4* • *257 404444* • *www.bestwestern.com* • *No air conditioning* • **KKKK**

9 Radisson SAS Alcron
In the 1930s, the Alcron was Prague's answer to New York's Ritz. The Radisson hotel group has carefully revived the hotel's Art Nouveau dandiness, besmirched by 40 years of secret police surveillance. There are two excellent restaurants on site. ◈ *Štěpánská 40* • *Map F5* • *222 820000* • *www.radisson.com/praguecs* • *Dis. access* • **KKKKK**

10 Comfort Hotel Prague
Located well outside the centre, the Comfort is nearer Ruzyně airport (see p126) than downtown. There are 131 basic but clean rooms, all with satellite TV, and there's a useful on-site car park and fitness centre with sauna. ◈ *Mrkvičkova 2, Prague 5* • *235 321060* • *www.fortunahotels.cz* • *No air conditioning* • **KK**

Left **Hotel Metamorphis** Right **Hotel Ungelt**

Old Town Hotels

Casa Marcello
Casa Marcello's elegantly appointed rooms embrace their 12th-century character; wandering the hotel's many stairs and hallways, you'll think you're in an Escher print. There is a small fitness club and excellent restaurant on the premises. ⓢ *Řásnovka 783 • Map N1 • 222 310260 • www.casa-marcello.cz • KKKKK*

Inter-Continental
The Inter-Continental pulls out all the stops for its Club-Level guests, but all visitors will feel pampered. The large fitness centre has exercise machines, a swimming pool and a putting green. On a budget? Rooms with city views are less expensive than those overlooking the Vltava. ⓢ *Náměstí Curieových 5 • Map E1 • 296 631111 • www.interconti.com • KKKK*

Černá liška
Across the street from Franz Kafka's birthplace, with unobstructed views of St Nicholas and Týn churches, the Black Fox is the only hotel on Old Town Square. There are more graceful places to stay, but few as well situated. Only 12 rooms, so book early. ⓢ *Mikulášská 2 • Map M3 • 224 322250 • www.cernaliska.cz • No air conditioning • KKKK*

U Zlaté studny
You'll tell the folks back home about this one. With its antique rooms and legendary cellar (ask about the well) the Golden Well is a luxurious adventure. Kids under 15 stay free. (Not to be confused with the hotel of the same name in Malá Strana.) ⓢ *Karlova 3 • Map K5 • 222 220262 • www.uzlatestudny.cz • KKKK*

Hotel Metamorphis
Stylish touches like parquet floors, tiled stoves and stirring views of Ungelt courtyard and the intricate façade of St James set the Metamorphis apart. No lift. The patio restaurant does big business in summer. ⓢ *Malá Štupartská 5 • Map N3 • 221 771011 • www.metamorphis.cz • KKKK*

U Medvídků
An excellent location, not only is the *pension* at the Bears centrally located, it's close to tram and metro stations, and situated above the city's favourite Budvar pub. ⓢ *Na Perštýně 7 • Map L6 • 224 211916 • www.umedviku.cz • No air conditioning • KKK*

Hotel Ungelt
The immediate vicinity is haunted by at least two ghosts, but guests at the Ungelt have registered no complaints. Perhaps they're sleeping too soundly in the nine renovated 10th-century apartments to notice. The courtyard offers glimpses of Týn Church. Book early. ⓢ *Malá Štupartská 1 • Map N3 • 224 828686 • www.ungelt.cz • No air conditioning • KKKKK*

Hotel Clementin
The Clementin has the peculiar honour of being the narrowest building in the city. As you might expect, the nine rooms in this Gothic building are small, but gracious. You might have trouble with large luggage. ⓢ *Seminářská 4 • Map K4 • 222 221798 • www.clementin.cz • No air conditioning • KKKK*

Hotel U staré paní
A no-frills affair, but the clean, modern building is staffed with an amiable crew. Each of the 18 rooms has a minibar and satellite TV, but for better entertainment, catch the acts at the club downstairs. ⓢ *Michalská 9 • Map L5 • 224 228090 • www.ustarepani.cz • No air conditioning • KKKK*

Hotel Josef
Modern and trendy in design, Hotel Josef fits in with Prague's new urban chic image with its simple clean-cut interiors and spacious rooms. ⓢ *Rybná 20 • Map N2 • 221 700901 • www.hoteljosef.com • KKK*

Note: Unless otherwise stated, all hotels accept credit cards, and have en-suite bathrooms and air conditioning

★★★★
ČERTOVKA
HOTEL

Above **Hotel Čertovka**

🔟 Malá Strana and Hradčany Hotels

1 U Tří Pštrosů
The hotel at the Three Ostriches gets its name from a 15th-century owner, who was a purveyor of ostrich feathers. The rooms are comfortably furnished and extremely quiet considering their proximity to Charles Bridge.
Ⓢ *Dražického náměstí 12* • Map D3 • 257 88888 • *www.upstrosu.cz* • *No air conditioning* • **KKKKK**

2 Rezidence Lundborg
In case the Charles Bridge view isn't enough, each of the 13 suites is equipped with a computer. The attic apartment features a fireplace and Jacuzzi. In the cellar, you'll find the Judith Bridge's foundations.
Ⓢ *U lužického semináře 3* • Map D2 • 257 011911 • *www.lundborg.cz* • **KKKKK**

3 Hotel Čertovka
You can watch boats pass under Charles Bridge on the Čertovka canal from windows overlooking Prague's "Little Venice". Top floor rooms have views of the castle. Parking is some distance from the hotel.
Ⓢ *U lužického semináře 2* • Map D2 • 257 011500 • *www.certovka.cz* • *No air conditioning* • **KKKKK**

4 Hotel Sax
Tucked into the heart of Malá Strana, the modern Sax is close to the Church of St Nicholas, the Church of Our Lady Victorious and Prague Castle. The 19 rooms and three suites surround a bright central atrium. Ⓢ *Jánský vršek 3* • Map B3 • 257 531268 • *www.sax.cz* • *No air conditioning* • **KKK**

5 Hotel Waldstein
Adjoining Duke Albrecht von Wallenstein's palace on a quiet courtyard, this cosy hotel features nine apartments and four double rooms. The rooms are extremely homey and furnished with antiques and reproductions. Ⓢ *Valdštejnske nám. 6* • Map C2 • 257 533938 • *www.avehotels.cz* • *No air conditioning* • **KKKKK**

6 Zlatá Hvězda
Built in 1327 as the residence of Hradčany's mayor, the Golden Star has a long history of elegance. The rooms and apartments are decked out with period furniture and modern baths. Room No. 33 is sublime.
Ⓢ *Nerudova 48* • Map C2 • 257 532867 • *www.hotelgoldenstar.com* • *No air conditioning* • **KKKKK**

7 Biskupský dům
The Bishop's House actually occupies two buildings: one is the Prague bishop's former residence; the other was a butcher's in the 18th century. Between them are 45 rooms, all comfortable and tastefully furnished. Ⓢ *Dražického náměstí 6* • Map D3 • 257 532320 • *www.hotelbishopshouse.com* • *No air conditioning* • **KKKKK**

8 Dům U Červeného Lva
From the House at the Red Lion, guests can see either Prague Castle and Nerudova to the north or Petřín Hill to the south. Guests will find it hard to leave room No. 32. Ⓢ *Nerudova 41* • Map C2 • 257 533833 • *www.hotelredlion.com* • *No air conditioning* • **KKKKK**

9 Domus Henrici
Built in 1372 on the steep hill overlooking the city, this small hotel is a stone's throw from Prague Castle. Each of the nine rooms has views of Petřín Hill and thoughtful amenities such as rocking chairs.
Ⓢ *Loretánská 11* • Map B2 • 220 511369 • *www.domus-henrici.cz* • *No air conditioning* • **KKKK**

10 Aria
An unusual little hotel, where each of the rooms, though not large, are modelled to a particular musical legend, be it Dizzy Gillespie or Mozart. The hotel's musical director will also advise you on concerts you can attend. Ⓢ *Tržiště 9* • Map C3 • 225 334111 • *www.ariahotel.net* • **KKKK**

Left **Doorman, Hotel Palace** Right **Hotel Evropa**

🔟 New Town Hotels

Hotel Palace
As classy as the hotels around the corner on Wenceslas Square, the Palace is renowned for its excellent service. The hotel offers several packages, including a two-day honeymoon deal, complete with tours and other extras. Little luxuries include marble-lined bathrooms. ◈ *Panská 12 • Map N5 • 224 093111 • www.palacehotel.cz • Dis. access* • **KKKKK**

Hotel Jalta
This Wenceslas Square designer hotel offers 89 stylish rooms and five luxurious suites. The restaurant serves an odd combination of traditional Bohemian and Japanese cuisine. Nice touches include the nursery and on-site dry cleaners. ◈ *Václavské náměstí 45 • Map N6 • 222 822111 • www.jalta.cz • Dis. access* • **KKKKK**

Hotel 16 U sv Kateřiny
The hotel at St Catherine's luxuriously furnished rooms and apartments are great value. Located near the Prague Botanical Gardens and the river, the family-run inn is very quiet and has little eccentricities like the display of lovely junk from the bazaar next door. ◈ *Kateřinská 16 • Map F6 • 224 919676 • www.hotel16.cz • Dis. access* • **KKK**

Hotel Axa
The Functionalist building dates from the 1930s. The interior is simple, with plenty of sunlight. Best are the sixth-floor rooms, which give you a view of Prague Castle. The pool in the basement is separately owned and hotel guests must pay to swim laps. ◈ *Na Poříčí 40 • Map G2 • 224 812580 • www.hotelaxa.com • No air conditioning* • **KKK**

Hotel Adria
In the 14th century, Carmelite nuns serving at the Church of Our Lady of the Snows had their convent on this site. The 88 snug rooms look out on either the Franciscan Gardens or busy Wenceslas Square, with its many shops, cinemas and cafés. Guarded parking nearby. ◈ *Václavské náměstí 26 • Map N6 • 221 081111 • www.adria.cz* • **KKKK**

Hotel Opera
The rooms at the Hotel Opera don't live up to the hot-pink neo-Renaissance façade. They are, however, great value, bright and comfortable. Particularly charming are No. 107, with its Mucha prints and pink velvet daybed, and the corner room No. 106, with its large bath. ◈ *Těšnov 13 • Map H1 • 222 315609 • www.hotel-opera.cz • No air conditioning* • **KKK**

Hotel Evropa
Despite the Art Nouveau façade and café, guests may miss modern conveniences; not all have en-suite bathrooms. The interior is somewhat outdated but first- and second-floor rooms have good views over Wenceslas Square. ◈ *Václavské náměstí 25 • Map P6 • 224 228117 • www.evropahotel.cz • No air conditioning* • **KKK**

Novoměstský Hotel
A bit old fashioned, but the staff try very hard. Close to Karlovo Náměstí and the New Town Hall. ◈ *Řeznická 4 • Map F5 • 222 231498 • www.novomestskyhotel.cz • No air conditioning* • **KKK**

Hotel Icon
This boutique hotel offers natural handmade beds from Sweden in every room. An oriental massage centre enhances its chic image. ◈ *V jámě 6 • Map F4 • 221 634100 • www.iconhotel.eu* • **KKK**

Na zlatém kříži
This charming hotel is situated in close proximity to Wenceslas Square. It offers a range of facilities, double rooms and apartments. This is a family-run hotel in a prime location. ◈ *Jungmannovo nàmesti 2 • 224 219501 • www.goldencross.cz* • **KKK**

➡ ***Note:** Unless otherwise stated, all hotels accept credit cards, and have en-suite bathrooms and air conditioning*

Price Categories

For a standard, double room per night (with breakfast if included), taxes and extra charges.

K	under Kč1,500
KK	Kč1,500–Kč3,000
KKK	Kč3,000–Kč4,500
KKKK	Kč4,500–Kč6,000
KKKKK	over Kč6,000

Above **Boatel Albatros**

🔟 Novelty Hotels

1 Hotel Kafka
The name may evoke some anxiety, but no guests at the sedate Kafka have woken to find themselves metamorphosed into beetles. The apartments can accommodate up to seven people. Good value. 🅂 *Cimburkova 24, Žižkov • Map B6 • 224 225769 • No air conditioning •* **KK**

2 Botel Racek
Floating on the Vltava's right bank, near the local yacht club and the city's large swimming and diving arena, the Racek offers 70 rooms, a restaurant and a top-deck disco. Nearby trams will take you to the centre in 10 minutes. 🅂 *Na Dvorecké louce, Podolí • 241 431628 • www.botelracek.cz • No air conditioning •* **KK**

3 Botel Albatros
The Albatros fancies itself romantic; enjoying a drink on the deck, gazing at Prague Castle you'd be inclined to agree. Old Town Square is a 10-minute walk away. The cabins are small, as befits a boat, but cosy. 🅂 *Nábřeží Ludvíka Svobody • 224 810547 • www.botelalbatros.cz • No air conditioning •* **KK**

4 Botel Admiral
Moored across the river from Palackého náměstí and the modern spires of Emmaus Monastery, the Admiral offers 84 tiny rooms.

Travellers who prefer more space should book one of the four apartments. Laundry and dry-cleaning services. 🅂 *Hořejší nábřeží, Smíchov • Map A6 • 257 321302 • www.admiral-botel.cz • No air conditioning •* **KK**

5 Hotel Cloister Inn
The Jesuits founded the cloister that gives the hotel its name. They were followed by the Grey Sisters of St Francis, who were in turn replaced by the secret police. The 73 rooms are somewhat joyless, but are good value for the neighbourhood. 🅂 *Konviktská 14 • Map K6 • 224 211020 • www.cloister-inn.com •* **KKK**

6 Hotel Expo'
Near Stromovka park, the Expo' was built to accommodate visitors attending trade fairs at the adjacent exhibition grounds. The 105 rooms each have satellite TV, video and minibar. Unwind in the sauna or have a massage. 🅂 *Za elektrárnou 3, Holešovice • Map B5 • 266 712470 • www.expoprag.cz • Dis. access •* **KKKK**

7 Hotel Pyramida
This large hotel near Prague Castle resembles an Aztec pyramid. Trams stopping outside whisk guests along a scenic route to the city centre in minutes. There's a large fitness centre on the premises as well as

hairdressers, a florist and a cinema. 🅂 *Bělohorská 24 • Map B2 • 233 355109 • www.hotelpyramida.cz • No air conditioning •* **KKK**

8 Hotel Squash
The hotel sits in a picturesque valley on the city's southern edge, near the confluence of the Berounka and the Vltava. Among the rooms, those in the garret are especially charming. 🅂 *K Cementárně 1427, Radotín • 257 912024 • recepce@hotelsquash.cz • No air conditioning •* **KK**

9 Hotel Yasmin
This hotel has been designed with luxury in mind, with 198 rooms over seven floors. Tasteful furnishings adorn each of the rooms and a '70s-retro globe hangs in the lobby. A summer terrace and the light airy feel offer a distinct difference from nearby offerings. 🅂 *Politických vězňů 12 • Map P6 • 234 100100 • www.hotel-yasmin.cz •* **KK**

10 Domeček ve Střešovicích
Situated in a country setting just a 15-minute walk from Prague Castle. The attic bedroom is furnished with antiques. Available only from March through October. Minimum three-night stay. 🅂 *Pod novým lesem 23, Střešovice • 233 920120 • interacta@vol.cz • No air conditioning •* **KK**

Left **Hostel ELF** Right **Hostel Advantage**

Hostels

Hostel Sokol
This central Malá Strana hostel takes its name from a First Republic national fitness movement. The six doubles and eight 12-bed rooms are up a suitably athletic flight of stairs. No smoking. ◎ *Nosticova 2 • Map D3 • 257 007397 • www.sokol-cos.cz • No air conditioning • K*

Travellers' Hostel
This company has more than 10 years' experience hosting wanderers in a network of hostels. This Old Town hostel is above the Roxy nightclub, but keep your carousing to a minimum, since you share the building with anxious neighbours. Other locations around town are open during the summer. ◎ *Dlouhá 33 • Map M2 • 224 826662 • www.travellers.cz • No air conditioning • K*

Hotel Imperial
The Imperial was an elegant hotel of the First Republic. However, owing to the difficulties of refitting a historic monument, the owner has chosen to recast it as a hostel. There's no longer anything posh about the rooms, which range from singles to quadruples, but the place has charm. ◎ *Na Poříčí 15 • Map G2 • 222 316012 • www.hotel-imperial.cz • No air conditioning • KK*

Sir Toby's Hostel
The staff here go to great lengths to be hospitable, throwing the occasional barbecue and helping travellers find other accommodation when the hostel is full. The bedrooms, baths and kitchen are immaculate. ◎ *Dělnická 24, Holešovice • Map B5 • 283 870635 • www.sirtobys.com • Dis. access • No air conditioning • No credit cards • K*

Boathouse Hostel
Located 20 minutes south of the centre and run by strict rules, the Boathouse is not a party hostel. It does, however, offer numerous services, such as laundry, internet access and bicycle and boat rental. Three to nine beds to a room. ◎ *Lodnická 1 • 415 658580 • www.hostelboathouse.com • No air conditioning • No credit cards • K*

Hostel Klub Habitat
The dormitory-style accommodation, with four to six beds to a room, is basic, but includes little niceties like fresh lemonade and snacks. ◎ *Na Zderaze 10 • Map E5 • 224 918252 • www.hostelz.com • No air conditioning • No credit cards • K*

Miss Sophie's
Located just a stone's throw from the centre, this is an ideal base to explore the city. It offers dorms as well as private rooms with en-suite bathrooms. Slightly more expensive are the apartments, complete with kitchen. ◎ *Melounova 3 • Map G6 • 296 303530 • www.miss-sophies.com • No air conditioning • No credit cards • K*

Hostel ELF
On the second floor of a *fin de siècle* building near the main bus and train stations, Hostel ELF's rooms range from singles to six-bed dormitories. There is a shared kitchen, common room and garden. The staff will arrange walking tours for you. ◎ *Husitská 11 • Map H3 • 222 540963 • www.hostelelf.com • No credit cards • No air conditioning • K*

Hostel Advantage
Accommodation ranges from singles to seven-bed rooms. Each floor has two kitchens and a TV room. ◎ *Sokolská 11–13 • Map G5 • 224 914062 • www.advantagehostel.cz • No air conditioning • K*

Hostel Estec Strahov
The dormitories are student housing through the school year. There is a beer garden adjacent Open July to September. ◎ *Vaníčkova 5, Strahov • Map A4 • 257 210410 • interacta@vol.cz • No air conditioning • K*

Recommend your favourite hostel on traveldk.com

Above left **Pension Cora** Right **Pension Denisa**

⭕🔟 Pensions and Bed-and-Breakfasts

1 U Raka

Prague's most romantic address, the House at the Crayfish started out as a barn in 1739. Inside the log walls are charming country-style rooms. Room No. 6 has its own garden, fireplace and well. Near Prague Castle and the Loreto. No children under 12. ◎ *Černínská 10 • Map A2 • 220 511100 • www. romantikhotel-uraka.cz* • **KKKKK**

2 Pension Dientzenhofer

The quiet house on the banks of the Čertovka canal is the birthplace of architect Kilian Ignaz Dientzenhofer, who built the nearby Church of St Nicholas and other Baroque edifices. The garden is idyllic. Very hospitable. ◎ *Nosticova 2 • Map D3 • 257 311319 • www.dientzenhofer.cz* • **KKK**

3 Pension Salieri

Just around the corner from Charles Bridge, this modest guesthouse is in the heart of Old Town. Very lively. ◎ *Liliová 18 • Map K5 • 222 220196 • www. gastroinfo.cz/salieri • No air conditioning* • **K**

4 Pension Vyšehrad

This lovely guesthouse is nearly inside the Vyšehrad walls. Stroll through the park each evening at sunset or sit in the pension's stunning garden. The four rooms are simply and comfortably furnished. Good access to public transport. Pets stay free. ◎ *Krokova 6 • Map B6 • 241 408455 • www. pension-vysehrad.cz • No air conditioning* • **K**

5 Pension Cora

Located in a peaceful villa-quarter in southeast Prague, the Cora is not central, but nearby buses and the pension's cars can take you anywhere you need to go. Amenities include satellite TV and a billiard room. The hosts serve a big breakfast. ◎ *Ve Studeném 7a, Braník • 241 490004 • www.corahotel.cz • No air conditioning* • **KK**

6 Pension Denisa

Newly reconstructed to high standards, the Denisa sits in a quiet neighbourhood just steps from the metro. The 35 rooms each have refrigerator and satellite TV; plus, your hosts bring breakfast to your room. ◎ *Národní obrany 33, Dejvice • Map A5 • 233 340224 • denisa@ avetravel.cz • No air conditioning* • **KK**

7 Church Pension

The Evangelic Church of the Czech Brethren puts its hospitality skills to the test at this small guesthouse. The rooms are suitably austere; not all have en-suite baths. Being a Christian affair, you may encounter a prayer group in the common room. The hosts are very pleasant. ◎ *Jungmannova 9 • Map M6 • 296 245432 • www.churchpension.cz • No air conditioning* • **KK**

8 Čelakovskeho sady

Overlooking the small green surrounding the National Museum, this bed-and-breakfast is just a three-minute walk to Wenceslas Square. The homey apartments and rooms are fully furnished down to the pots and pans. ◎ *Čelakovského sady 8 • Map G5 • 257 210410 • interacta@vol.cz • No air conditioning* • **KK**

9 Pension Standard

First-rate accommodation in a Jugendstil house along the Vltava. Nine double rooms and two suites. Guests make use of a private garage. Children under seven stay free. ◎ *Rašínovo nábřeží 38 • Map B6 • 224 916060 • www.standard.cz* • **KK**

10 Hotel Marit

Situated in a residential neighbourhood, the Marit feels like a family home. All rooms have satellite TV. Kids under 10 stay half-price. ◎ *Čapkova 13, Michle • 261 223842 • www. hotelmarit.cz • No air conditioning* • **KK**

Left **Residence Řetězová** Right **House at the "New World"**

Apartments

1 Apartment Lužická

This spacious, one-bedroom flat on a tree-lined Vinohrady street is tastefully appointed with simple furniture. The bright kitchen has all the utensils you need, a stocked refrigerator and a washing machine. ◈ *Lužická 14, Vinohrady • Map B6 • 251 512502 • info@prague accommodations.com • No air conditioning • KKK*

2 Residence Řetězová

A palace historically known as the House at the Three Golden Chains has been converted into nine spacious apartments. Each has vaulted ceilings, wooden floors and Italian baths. The Old Town location can't be beat. ◈ *Řetězova 9 • Map K5 • 222 221800 • www.residenceretezova.com • KKK*

3 The House at the "New World"

A private residence in this gorgeous lane behind the castle is the dream of many Prague residents. The large house is bright and thoroughly modern inside, with three bedrooms, two baths, fully equipped kitchen and a large living room with fireplace. Central gas heating. ◈ *Nový Svět 15 • Map A2 • 233 920118 • interacta@vol.cz • No air conditioning • KK*

4 Apartments Vlašská

Four romantic and newly renovated apartments on a palace-lined Malá Strana street, each with beautiful painted wooden beams, large windows, antique furniture and modern baths. ◈ *Vlašská 7–8 • Map B3 • 233 920118 • interacta@vol.cz • Dis. access • No air conditioning • KKK*

5 Residence Nosticova

Tucked into a hidden corner of Malá Strana, the Nosticova is popular with film stars and other VIPs. The apartments are decked out with such fine touches as antique clocks and crystal chandeliers. All this, and it's just a few minutes' walk from Charles Bridge. ◈ *Nosticova 1 • Map D3 • 257 312513 • www.nosticova.com • No air conditioning • KKKKK*

6 Villa Franklin D Roosevelt

Formerly the US cultural attaché's residence, the Roosevelt is located in Prague's elegant diplomatic district. There are three luxurious Art Deco apartments, a sauna, steam bath and, for secret agent types, bulletproof cars and bodyguards for hire. ◈ *Rooseveltova 18, Bubeneč • Map A5 • 224 310478 • www.villa-roosevelt.cz • No air conditioning • Dis. access • KKKK*

7 Apartments Slezská

This booking agency offers three apartments at this address near metro and tram stops. Fully equipped kitchens, TVs and carpets help make guests comfortable. ◈ *Slezská 23, Vinohrady • Map B6 • 233 920118 • interacta@vol.cz • No air conditioning • K*

8 The Castle Steps

These apartments and rooms make you feel like a pampered guest who has just entered a stately home. All of the bright rooms are furnished with period features and many have views over the city and Petřín park. ◈ *Nerudova 7 • Map C2 • 257 216337 • www.castlesteps.com • KKK*

9 Privát Pankrác

This large third-floor flat comprises two bedrooms, bath, kitchen, TV and stereo. Stay more than 7 nights and your transport to and from the airport is free. ◈ *Na Jezerce 9, Pankrác • www.hotelsprague.cz/pankrac • No air conditioning • K*

10 Pension Klenor

Five kilometres (3 miles) from the city centre. There are 10 rooms, each with its own bath and satellite TV. Outdoor swimming pool. ◈ *Ve Studeném 6, Braník • 241 723240 • No air conditioning • KK*

Many apartments have a minimum stay of at least three nights or one week – check when making a booking.

Price Categories

For a standard,	**K**	under Kč1,500
double room per	**KK**	Kč1,500–Kč3,000
night (with breakfast	**KKK**	Kč3,000–Kč4,500
if included), taxes	**KKKK**	Kč4,500–Kč6,000
and extra charges.	**KKKKK**	over Kč6,000

Above **Hotel Anna**

⑩ Hotels outside the City Centre

① Hotel Diplomat
Near, but not within earshot of Ruzyně airport, the Diplomat has 388 rooms and all modern conveniences. Facilities include several restaurants, a business centre and an indoor go-cart track. Children under six stay free. Good access to the centre. ⌕ *Evropská 15, Dejvice • Map A5 • 296 559111 • www.diplomathotel.cz • Dis. access* • **KKK**

② Dorint Don Giovanni Prague
The Don Giovanni offers excellent value in the form of its 400 elegant rooms and 43 suites. Guests can take advantage of the spa-treatment facilities and baby-sitting service. The hotel is conveniently located near metro, bus and tram stops. ⌕ *Vinohradská 157, Žižkov • Map B6 • 267 031111 • www.dorint.de/Prag • Dis. access* • **KKKK**

③ Hotel Praha
The Communists secluded this wave-shaped modern master-piece within its own park. The Party would blush to see the bourgeoisie enjoying the hotel's gourmet restaurant and brasserie, swimming pool and tennis courts. The rooms are as fine as any in town. ⌕ *Sušická 20, Dejvice • Map A5 • 224 341111 • www.htlpraha.cz • Dis. access* • **KKKKK**

④ Hotel Belvedere
Located near Veletržní Palace *(see pp26–7)*, the Belvedere is a short walk to the Old Town or Prague Castle. Trams stop just outside. The rooms are a bit dreary, however. ⌕ *Milady Horákové 19, Holešovice • Map B5 • 220 106111 • www.belvedere-hotel. com • Dis. access* • **KKK**

⑤ Hotel Sieber
Built in 1889 as a block of flats, the Sieber has had a rocky history. A US bombing raid damaged it in 1945. Nationalized after World War II, it didn't return to the Sieber family hands until 1991. Not elegant, but the staff are delightful. ⌕ *Slezská 55, Žižkov • Map B6 • 224 250025 • www.sieber.cz* • **KKKK**

⑥ Hotel Anna
The Art Nouveau building in Vinohrady was built as a private residence at the end of the 19th century. The 22 rooms are decorated with engravings of historic Prague. From the top-floor suites, you can enjoy views of the castle and the Old Town. ⌕ *Budečská 17 • Map B6 • 222 513111 • www. hotelanna.cz • Dis. access • No air conditioning* • **KK**

⑦ Hotel Vyšehrad
Between Wenceslas Square and the monuments of Vyšehrad, this hotel is fully up to date with satellite TV and internet connections but holds on to its 19th-century charm. ⌕ *Marie Cibulkové 29, Vyšehrad • Map B6 • 261 225592 • www.hotelvysehrad.cz* • **KKK**

⑧ Hotel Excellent
This small hotel lives up to its name if you don't mind being away from the crowd. Your hosts are happy to book flights, train tickets, seats at the opera or just show you around town. ⌕ *Líbeznická 164/19, Kobylisy • 284 687295 • www.hotel-excellent.cz • No air conditioning* • **KK**

⑨ Hotel Julián
Within walking distance of Malá Strana, the Julián is an Art Nouveau charmer. Guests will gush over the red-velvet lift and the fireside library. Suite No. 402 has a kitchen and there is a business centre and conference room. ⌕ *Eliśky Peškové 11, Smíchov • Map A6 • 257 311150 • www.julian.cz • Dis. access* • **KK**

⑩ Hotel Vaníček
Overlooking Smíchov from its perch on Petřín Hill, the Vaníček offers guests a river view from its terraces. Simple rooms and services. ⌕ *Na Hřebenkách 60, Smíchov • Map A6 • 257 320414 • www.hotel vanicek.cz • No air conditioning* • **KKK**

General Index

Acknowledgements

Main Contributor

Theodore Schwinke moved to the Czech Republic from the United States in 1996. A former editor of *The Prague Post*, his current projects include a children's book on the 16th-century Danish astronomer Tycho Brahe and a book on St Gorazd of Prague.

Produced by Sargasso Media Ltd, London

Project Editor
Zoë Ross
Art Editor
Philip Lord
Picture Research
Rhiannon Furbear, Helen Stallion
Proofreader
Stewart J Wild
Indexer
Hilary Bird
Editorial Assistance
Jakub Sverák

Main Photographer
Nigel Hudson

Additional Photography
Jiři Doležal, Jiři Kopřiva, Vladimir Kozlik, František Přeučil, Milan Posselt, Stanislav Tereba, Peter Wilson

Illustrator
chrisorr.com

For Dorling Kindersley
Publishing Manager
Marisa Renzullo
Publisher
Douglas Amrine
Senior Cartographic Editor
Casper Morris
DTP
Jason Little
Production
Melanie Dowland
Picture Librarians
Hayley Smith, David Saldanha

Maps
Dominic Beddow, Simonetta Giori (Draughtsman Ltd)

Additional Editorial Assistance
Emma Anacootee, Sherry Collins, Michelle Crane, Tomás Kleisner, Maite Lantaron, Marianne Petrou, Beth Potter, Quadrum Solutions, Sands Publishing Solutions, Sadie Smith, Leah Tether, Conrad van Dyk

Picture Credits
t-top, tl-top left; tlc-top left centre; tc-top centre; tr-top right; cla-centre left above; ca-centre above; cra-centre right above; cl-centre left; c-centre; cr-centre right; clb-centre left below; cb-centre below; crb-centre right below; bl-bottom left, b-bottom; bc-bottom centre; bcl-bottom centre left; br-bottom right; d-detail.

Acknowledgements

Every effort has been made to trace the copyright holders of images, and we apologize in advance for any unintentional omissions. We would be pleased to insert the appropriate acknowledgements in any subsequent edition of this publication.

The publishers would like to thank the following individuals, companies, and picture libraries for permission to reproduce their photographs:

AKG London: 11, 34tr, 35tl, 35 tr, 44tl, 44tc, 45tl, 45tr, 53t, Eric Lessing: 34b, 44b;

BOHEMIA BAGEL: 88tl; CAFÉ SLAVIA: 60cla; CORBIS: 35bl, 44tr; LA CREPERIE: 122tl CZECH TOURIST AUTHORITY: 1, 20–21, 70–71, 72tr, 73t, 90tl, 92t, 93r, 108–109, 114tl, 118–19;

CTK CZECH NEWS AGENCY: 4–5, 7t, 52tc, 52tr, 55br, 68tl, 68tr, 68c, 69bl, 69r, 76tr, 91t, 94–95, 115b, 116, 117t, 122tr, 135tr; FORTEAN PICTURE LIBRARY: 52tl; RUUD JONKERS: 47r; KAPLAN PRODUCTIONS: 25, 35br, 45br, 52b; ;Courtesy of THE KOBAL COLLECTION: Mandalay Entertainment 46b; Paramount Pictures 46tl; Portobello Pictures/Biograf Jan Sverak 46tr; Saul Zaenz Compnay 47tl; NATIONAL GALLERY OF PRAGUE: Paul Cézanne *House at Aix*, 1885-7 26c, Eugene Delacroix *Jaguar Attacking Horseman*, 27t, Paul Gaugin *Bonjour, Monsieur Gaugin*, 18, 26b, Vincent Van Gogh *Green Wheat*, 1889, 27b, Otto Gutfreund *Anxiety*, 1912–13, 7c, 27cr, Karlovy Lázné 66tl, 77tl; August Rodin *St John the Baptist*, 1878, 27c; RADISSON SAS ALCRON HOTEL: 62tl; IL RITROVO: 123 THE RONALD GRANT ARCHIVE: Orion 46cl; ZAHRADA v OPÉRE: 113tl

Phrase Book

In an Emergency

Help!	**Pomoc!**	po-mots
Stop!	**Zastavte!**	za-stav-te
Call a doctor!	**Zavolejte doktora!**	za-vo-ley-te dok-to-ra!
Call an ambulance!	**Zavolejte sanitku!**	za-vo-ley-te sa-nit-ku!
Call the police!	**Zavolejte policii!**	za-vo-ley-te poli-tsi-yi!
Call the fire brigade!	**Zavolejte hasiče**	za-vol-ey-te ha-si-che
Where is the telephone?	**Kde je telefón?**	gde ye tele-fohn?
the nearest hospital?	**nejbližší nemocnice?**	ney-blish-ee ne-mots-nyitse?

Communication Essentials

Yes/No	**Ano/Ne**	ano/ne
Please	**Prosím**	pro-seem
Thank you	**Děkuji vám**	dye-ku-ji vahm
Excuse me	**Prosím vás**	pro-seem vahs
Hello	**Dobrý den**	do-bree den
Goodbye	**Na shledanou**	na s-hle-da-no
Good evening	**Dobrý večer**	dob-ree vech-er
morning	**ráno**	rah-no
afternoon	**odpoledne**	od-po-led-ne
evening	**večer**	ve-cher
yesterday	**včera**	vche-ra
today	**dnes**	dnes
tomorrow	**zítra**	zeet-ra
here	**tady**	ta-di
there	**tam**	tam
What?	**Co?**	tso?
When?	**Kdy?**	gdi?
Why?	**Proč?**	proch?
Where?	**Kde?**	gde?

Useful Phrases

How are you?	**Jak se máte?**	yak-se mah-te?
Very well, thank you.	**Velmi dobře děkuji**	vel-mi dob-rzhe dye kuyi
Pleased to meet you	**Těší mě**	tyesh-ee mye
See you soon	**Uvidíme se brzy**	u-vi-dyee-me-se-brzy
That's fine	**To je v pořádku**	to ye vpo-rzhahdku
Where is/are...?	**Kde je/jsou ...?**	gde ye/yso ...?
How long does it take to get to...?	**Jak dlouho to trvá se dostat do...?**	yak dlo ho to tr-va se do-stat do...?
How do I get to...?	**Jak se dostanu k ...?**	yak se do-sta-nu k
Do you speak English?	**Mluvíte anglicky?**	mlu-vee-te an-glits-ki?
I don't understand	**Nerozumím**	ne-ro-zu-meem
Could you speak more slowly?	**Mohl(a)* byste mluvit trochu pomaleji?**	mohl- (a) bis-te mlu-vit tro-khu po-maley?
Pardon?	**Prosím?**	pro-seem?
I'm lost	**Ztratil(a)* jsem se**	stra-tyil (a) ysem se

Useful Words

big	**velký**	vel-kee
small	**malý**	mal-ee
hot	**horký**	hor-kee
cold	**studený**	stu-den-ee
good	**dobrý**	dob-ree
bad	**špatný**	shpat-nee
well	**dobře**	dob-rzhe
open	**otevřeno**	ot-ev-rzhe-no
closed	**zavřeno**	zav-rzhe-no
left	**do leva**	do le-va
right	**do prava**	do pra-va
straight on	**rovně**	rov-nye
near	**blízko**	blee-sko
far	**daleko**	da-le-ko
up	**nahoru**	na-ho-ru
down	**dolů**	do-loo
early	**brzy**	br-zi
late	**pozdě**	poz-dye
entrance	**vchod**	vkhod
exit	**východ**	vee-khod

toilets	**toalety**	toa-leti
free, unoccupied	**volný**	vol-nee
free, no charge	**zdarma**	zdar-ma

Making a Telephone Call

I'd like to place a long-distance call	**Chtěl(a)* bych volat mezistátsky**	khtyel(a) bikh vo-lat i me-zi mye-stski
I'd like to make a reverse-charge call	**Chtěl(a)* bych volat na účet volaného**	khtyel(a) bikh volat na oo-chet volan-eh-ho
I'll try again later	**Zkusím to později**	skus-eem to poz-dyey
Can I leave a message?	**Mohu nechat zprávu?**	mo-hu ne-khat sprah-vu?
Hold on	**Počkejte**	poch-key-te
local call	**místní hovor**	meest-nyee hovor

Sightseeing

art gallery	**galerie**	ga-ler-riye
bus stop	**autobusová zastávka**	au-to-bus-o-vah za-stah-vka
church	**kostel**	kos-tel
garden	**zahrada**	za hra-da
library	**knihovna**	knyi-hov-na
museum	**muzeum**	muz-e-um
railway station	**nádraží**	nah-dra-zhee
tourist information	**turistické informace**	tooristi-tske in-for-ma-tse
closed for the public holiday	**státní svátek**	staht-nyee svah-tek

Shopping

How much does this cost?	**Co to stojí?**	tso to sto-yee?
I would like ...	**Chtěl(a)* bych ...**	khtyel(a) bikh...
Do you have ...?	**Máte ...?**	maa-te ...?
I'm just looking	**Jenom se dívám**	ye-nom se dyee-vahm
Do you take credit cards?	**Berete kreditní karty?**	be-re-te kred-it nyee karti?
What time do you open/close?	**V kolík otevíráte/zavíráte?**	v ko-lik o-te-vee-rah-te/za vee rah-te?
this one	**tento**	ten-to
that one	**tamten**	tam-ten
expensive	**drahý**	dra-hee
cheap	**levný**	lev-nee
size	**velikost**	vel-ik-ost
white	**bílý**	bee-lee
black	**černý**	cher-nee
red	**červený**	cher-ven-ee
yellow	**žlutý**	zhlu-tee
green	**zelený**	zel-en-ee
blue	**modrý**	mod-ree
brown	**hnědý**	hnyed-ee

Types of Shop

antiques shop	**starožitnictví**	sta-ro zhit-nyits-tvee
bank	**banka**	banka
bakery	**pekárna**	pe-kahr-na
bookstore	**knihkupectví**	knih-kupets-tvee
butcher	**řeznictví**	rzhez-nyits-tvee
chemist (prescriptions etc)	**lékárna**	leh-kah-rma
chemist (toiletries etc)	**drogerie**	drog-erye
delicatessen	**lahůdky**	la-hoo-dki
department store	**obchodní dům**	op-khod-nyee doom
grocery	**potraviny**	pot-ra-vini
glass	**sklo**	sklo
market	**trh**	trkh
newsstand	**novinový stánek**	no-vi-novee stah-nek
post office	**pošta**	posh-ta
supermarket	**samoobsluha**	sa-mo-ob-slu-ha
tobacconist	**tabák**	ta-bahk
travel agency	**cestovní kancelář**	tses-tov-nyi kantse-laarzh

PHRASE BOOK

Staying in a Hotel

Do you have a vacant room?	**Máte volný pokoj?**	mah-te vol-nee po-koy?
double room	**dvoulůžkový pokoj**	dvo-loozh-kovee po-koy
with double bed	**s dvojitou postelí**	sdvoy-to pos-telee
twin room	**pokoj s dvěma postelemi**	po-koy sdvye-ma pos-tel-emi
room with a bath	**pokoj s koupelnou**	po-koy s ko-pel-no
porter	**vrátný**	vraht-nee
I have a reservation	**Mám reservaci**	
mahm rez-ervatsi		

Eating Out

Have you got a …?	**Máte stůl pro …?**	mah-te stool pro
table for …?		
I'd like to reserve a table	**Chtěl(a)* bych rezervovat stůl**	khtyel(a) bikh rez-er-vov-at stool
breakfast	**snídaně**	snyee-danye
lunch	**oběd**	ob-yed
dinner	**večeře**	vech e-rzhe
The bill, please	**Prosím, účet**	pro-seem oo-chet
I am a vegetarian	**Jsem vegetarián(ka)***	ysem veghe-tariahn(ka)
waitress!	**slečno**	slech-no
waiter!	**pane vrchní!**	pane vrkh-nyee!
fixed-price menu	**standardní menu**	stan-dard-nyee
dish of the day	**nabídka dne**	nab-eed-ka dne
starter	**předkrm**	przhed-krm
main course	**hlavní jídlo**	hlav-nyee yeed-lo
vegetables	**zelenina**	zel-en-yin-a
dessert	**zákusek**	zah-kusek
cover charge	**poplatek**	pop-la-tek
wine list	**nápojový lístek**	nah-po-yo-vee lee-stek
rare (steak)	**krvavý**	kr-va-vee
medium	**středně udělaný**	strzhed-nye ud-yel-an-ee
well done	**dobře udělaný**	dobrzhe-ud-yel-an-ee
glass	**sklenice**	sklen-yitse
bottle	**láhev**	lah-hev
knife	**nůž**	noozh
fork	**vidlička**	vid-lich-ka
spoon	**lžíce**	lzhee-tse

Menu Decoder

biftek	bif-tek	steak
bílé víno	bee-leh vee-no	white wine
bramborové knedlíky	bram-bo-ro-veh kne-dleeki	potato dumplings
brambory	bram-bo-ri	potatoes
chléb	khlehb	bread
cibule	tsi-bu-le	onion
citrónový džus	tsi-tron-o-vee dzhuus	lemon juice
cukr	tsukr	sugar
čaj	chay	tea
čerstvé ovoce	cher-stveh-o-vo-ce	fresh fruit
červené víno	cher-ven-eh vee-no	red wine
česnek	ches-nek	garlic
dort	dort	cake
fazole	fa-zo-le	beans
grilované	gril-ov-a-neh	grilled
houby	ho-bi	mushrooms
houska	hous-ka	roll
houskové knedlíky	ho-sko-veh kne-dleeki	bread dumplings
hovězí	hov-ye-zee	beef
hranolky	hran-ol-ki	chips
husa	hu-sa	goose
jablko	ya-bl-ko	apple
jahody	ya-ho-di	strawberries
jehněčí	ye-hnye-chee	lamb
kachna	kakh-na	duck
kapr	ka-pr	carp
káva	kah-va	coffee
kuře	ku-rzhe	chicken
kyselé zelí	kis-el-eh zel-ee	sauerkraut
maso	ma-so	meat
máslo	mah-slo	butter
minerálka	min-er-ahl-ka	mineral water
šumivá/	shum-i-vah/	fizzy/
nešumivá	ne-shum i-vah	stilly

mléko	mleh-ko	milk
mořská jídla	morzh-skah-yeed-la	seafood
ocet	ots-et	vinegar
okurka	o-ku-rka	cucumber
olej	oley	oil
párek	paa-rek	sausage
pečené	petsh-en-eh	baked
pečené	pech-en-eh	roast
pepř	peprzh	pepper
polévka	pol-eh-vka	soup
pomeranč	po-me-ranch	orange
pomerančový džus	po-me-ran-ch– o-vee dzhuus	orange juice
pivo	pi-vo	beer
rajské	rayskeh	tomato
ryba	rib-a	fish
rýže	ree-zhe	rice
salát	sal-at	salad
sůl	sool	salt
sýr	seer	cheese
šunka	shun-ka	ham
vařená/	varzh-enah	cooked
uzená	u-zenah	smoked
telecí	te-le-tsee	veal
vajíčko	va-yee-chko	egg
vařené	varzh-en-eh	boiled
vepřové	vep-rzho-veh	pork
voda	vo-da	water
zelí	zel-ee	cabbage
zelenina	zel-enyina	vegetables
zmrzlina	zmrzl-in-a	ice cream

Numbers

1	**jedna**	yed-na
2	**dvě**	dvye
3	**tř**	itrzhi
4	**čtyři**	chti-rzhi
5	**pět**	pyet
6	**šest**	shest
7	**sedm**	sedm
8	**osm**	osm
9	**devět**	dev-yet
10	**deset**	des-et
11	**jedenáct**	ye-de-nahtst
12	**dvanáct**	dva-nahtst
13	**třináct**	trzhi-nahtst
14	**čtrnáct**	chtr-nahtst
15	**patnáct**	pat-nahtst
16	**šestnáct**	shest-nahtst
17	**sedmnáct**	sedm-nahtst
18	**osmnáct**	osm-nahtst
19	**devatenáct**	de-va-te-nahtst
20	**dvacet**	dva-tset
21	**dvacet jedna**	dva-tset yed-na
22	**dvacet dva**	dva-tset dva
30	**třicet**	trzhi-tset
40	**čtyřicet**	chti-rzhi-tset
50	**padesát**	pa-de-saht
60	**šedesát**	she-de-saht
70	**sedmdesát**	sedm-de-saht
80	**osmdesát**	osm-de-saht
90	**devadesát**	de-va-de-saht
100	**sto**	sto
1,000	**tisíc**	tyi-seets
2,000	**dva tisíce**	dva tyi-see-tse
5,000	**pět tisíc**	pyet tyi-seets
1,000,000	**milión**	mi-li-ohn

Time

one minute	**jedna minuta**	yed-na min-uta
one hour	**jedna hodina**	yed-na hod-yin-a
half an hour	**půl hodiny**	pool hod-yin-i
day	**den**	den
week	**týden**	tee-den
Monday	**pondělí**	pon-dye-lee
Tuesday	**Úterý**	oo-ter-ee
Wednesday	**středa**	strzhe-da
Thursday	**čtvrtek**	chtvr-tek
Friday	**pátek**	pah-tek
Saturday	**sobota**	so-bo-ta
Sunday	**neděle**	ned-yel-e